Charles Henry Corey

**A History of the Richmond Theological Seminary**

With Reminiscences of Thirty Years' Work Among the Colored People...

Charles Henry Corey

**A History of the Richmond Theological Seminary**
*With Reminiscences of Thirty Years' Work Among the Colored People...*

ISBN/EAN: 9783337000943

Printed in Europe, USA, Canada, Australia, Japan

Cover: Foto ©Lupo / pixelio.de

More available books at **www.hansebooks.com**

# A HISTORY

OF THE

# Richmond Theological Seminary,

WITH

## REMINISCENCES OF THIRTY YEARS' WORK

AMONG THE

COLORED PEOPLE OF THE SOUTH.

BY

CHARLES H. COREY,

President of Richmond Theological Seminary.

WITH AN

INTRODUCTION BY W. W. LANDRUM, D. D.

RICHMOND, VA.
J. W. RANDOLPH COMPANY.
1895.

# Table of Contents.

Chapter I.—Some Matters Personal—The United States Christian Commission—Schools for Colored Soldiers at Port Hudson—Getting out of the Red River..... 13

Chapter II.—Morris Island—Entry into Charleston—Incidents—A Sunrise Prayer-Meeting—The First Sermon—The Dead Officer—The Disgusted Officer—A Mock Auction—Incidents—The Old Flag Back—Resolutions—Departure ................................. 20

Chapter III.—Missionary Work in South Carolina—Condition of the Churches—Church Organized in the Woods—On the Sea Islands—Rev. T. Willard Lewis and Other Methodist Workers—Statistics—The Augusta Institute................................... 36

Chapter IV.—The Evacuation of Richmond—The Burning of the City—Mr. Lumpkin's Coffle of Slaves—Lecture by Dr. Burrows—President Lincoln in Richmond—Lumpkin's Jail—His Daughters in a Northern Seminary—Rev. Mr. Newman's Experience..... 42

Chapter V.—Condition of the Freedmen at the Close of the War—Work in their Behalf by the American Baptist Home Mission Society—Early Work in Richmond—The National Theological Institute and University—Dr. N. Colver—Dr. Robert Ryland—Dr. Parker's Lectures—Resolutions................ 51

## Table of Contents.

Chapter VI.—Dr. Colver's Work in Richmond—Letters—Transfer of the Work of the National Theological Institute and University to the American Baptist Home Mission Society—Report of Work Done...... 59

Chapter VII.—Letter of Dr. Simmons on Lumpkin's Jail—Recollections by Mrs. H. Goodman-Smith—Purchase of the United States Hotel—Incorporated as Richmond Institute.......................... 69

Chapter VIII.—Extracts from Official Letters of Secretaries—Extracts from other Letters—Needy Students................................................. 90

Chapter IX.—Need of Enlightened Leaders—Extracts from Letters—Difficulties—Early Encouragements—Drs. Dickinson and Jeter—Other early Friends—An Amusing Incident—The Capitol Disaster.......... 111

Chapter X—The Freedmen's Bureau—Act of Incorporation—Purchase of a New Site—A Higher Theological School Needed—The Richmond Theological Seminary Incorporated..................................... 123

Chapter XI.—Our Students—Results of Their Labor—Letters from Students............................... 135

Chapter XII.—Our Teachers—Sketches of Our Present Professors—Special Lectures—Occasional Lectures—Distinguished Visitors—Need of Endowment—Funds Secured—Attempted Removal..................... 173

Chapter XIII.—The Old African Church—A Historic Building—Its Religious History—Dr. Ryland's Pastorate—Pastorate of Rev. James H. Holmes........ 185

Chapter XIV.—The Slave as a Man—As a Christian—As a Soldier—As a Free Man—Statistics............... 198

CHAPTER XV.—Then—Now—Pleasant Recollections—Preaching to Phil. Kearney Post, G. A. R., and R. E. Lee Camp—Visits Abroad—Beneficiary Aid—The American Baptist Home Mission Society and its Workers...................................... 207

CHAPTER XVI.—Slow Progress—Our Ancestors—The Bible—Work for the Lowly—Suffrage—Conclusion.... 220

NOTES ............................................. 229

INDEX............................................. 233

# PREFACE.

The facts pertaining to the founding of any institution of learning are always of interest to those who live afterwards. The experiences through which the early laborers pass; their struggles and their triumphs are instructive and stimulating. What may seem unimportant and not out of the routine of our daily duty to-day, may be of intense interest, and also of profit to the generations that follow. This has always been the case in the founding and building up of the Colleges and Seminaries of our denomination.

In view of such considerations as these, it has been considered desirable to collect and record such facts concerning the early history of our beloved Richmond Theological Seminary, as it may be presumed will be of interest in the future to persons of all classes, whether in the North or in the South.

In the providence of God, the writer of this little volume has been permitted to continue in the work for the colored people from the close of the war to the present time. Twenty-seven years of this period has been spent in Richmond, once the Capital of the Southern Confederacy. This volume contains more than a mere history of the growth of the school itself; it treats of matters that may seem to some irrelevant and not germane to the subject. Yet, considering the transition period which followed the close of the war, and the feelings engendered by the changed relations of the white and colored races, it is quite impossible to restrict our statements to the mere details of the growth of the school from year to year. That this little book may be instructive to some, incidents in which the writer took part at the close of the war are referred to. Facts of interest and statistics are given. None of these points can be elaborated in a volume of this kind, and they can be only hinted at. Exacting professional duties have claimed the attention of the writer to so great a degree that only the mere fragments of time could be given to this work. Dr. Simmons and Dr. Morehouse have kindly consented to the publishing of extracts from their official correspondence. Drs. Parker, Peck, Backus, Taylor, Bishop, and Cutting, under all of whom the writer served officially, have passed away. He has not, therefore, felt at liberty to use many of their letters. In all letters from which extracts have been made, the desire has been to convey information, to enforce a point, or to teach a lesson.

Some portions of this book refer so exclusively to scenes in which the writer took part that they may appear to be immodestly personal. This could not well be avoided, and the writer begs that this defect may be overlooked. No attempt is here made to give a history of the great work done by Baptists for the colored people of the South. The origin and progress of their work is fully described in the publications which are issued, from time to time, by the American Baptist Home Mission Society, and by the other societies engaged in this work.

Rev. Charles Carleton Coffin, the "Carleton" of the Boston *Journal*, during the late war, from whose writings some extracts are made, is an author of note, and his works have been widely read.

Some statistics change with each passing year, and some of those which are given may not be fully up to date. Others, taken from the public press, cannot be properly verified, and may be exaggerated.

The Commissioner of Education and the War Department, at Washington, have kindly furnished information and statistics, and for this service acknowledgements are gratefully made.

It has been impossible to hear from all of our old students, and this part of the work is necessarily incomplete. The writer strove, through the public press and by circulars, to reach every ministerial student connected with the School from the year 1868 to the present year. Replies to the questions asked came to hand from about one in every ten. The address of many could not be ascertained. Many more, whose modesty prevented them from furnishing the desired information, have done a noble work for Christ, and are highly honored and greatly beloved. Many have finished their work and have gone to their reward.

No attempt has been made to tabulate the work or to sketch the career of a number of former pupils who have entered upon professional and business life. Some have already won for themselves distinction in the legal and medical professions. Others, as bankers, teachers and business men, are achieving success as well as proving themselves useful and valuable members of society.

If there be found in some of the extracts from the letters and writers quoted expressions and sentiments with which the reader cannot agree, it must be remembered that these are introduced. not to provoke controversy nor to engender strife, but for the purpose of furnishing information. He who would intentionally do anything to widen the breach between the two races is a friend to neither.

With thanks to all who have in any way contributed to make this little volume what it is, it is sent forth to the public with a desire that it may directly and indirectly promote the material and spiritual improvement of the people to whose upbuilding thirty of the best years of a lifetime have been given.

# INTRODUCTION.

As an usher, I gladly open the door for the readers of this volume. It is a simple story, simply told; it is a true story, truthfully told. It is not intended to occupy a large place in the great world of literature. The circle it addresses embraces those few choice spirits who are the conscientious and consistent friends of our "Brother in Black." That circle, whether we consider it as embracing those devoted to the religious or the educational, the political or the social well being of the American negro, has never been so large as it should be. Quality, rather than numbers, has marked it. The elect of God and the brothers to humanity, however, will read with throbbing hearts this interesting recital of self-sacrificing service for the lowly.

The historian of the future will need this book. It recounts, step by step, the course of progress the long subject race has pursued since the days of its emancipation. That progress, so rapid and marvellous, has delighted the friends and confounded the foes of its regeneration and uplifting. The human causes of that progress have been, not so much the enactments of Congress and of State Legislatures, as the benefactions of a few philanthropists and the gifts of a respectable number of earnest Christians who founded schools; and, most of all, the difficult, discriminating and self-forgetting exertions of the Christ-like men who have directed and taught in those schools.

The history of the Richmond Theological Seminary is a worthy history. Its teachers have been competent and well qualified; its course of study has been wide and thorough; its pupils have done well within its walls and even better beyond them; its atmosphere has been clean and pure; its influence has been for all that ennobles the colored man, without the slightest hostility to the white man. These pages will bring peculiar pleasure to the Seminary's many friends. They will add to the number of its friends. They will bless the souls of all who read them by drawing them nearer to the heart of Christ.

"As the pastor of the author for many years, I may be allowed to say that his pure life, his consecrated zeal, his sound judgment, his prudent counsel, his amiable temper and consummate tact have won for him the confidence and admiration of both races in this community. He has pursued the even tenor of his way between extremists, among both blacks and whites. Criticism has never discouraged him; condemnation could not cow his spirit; commendation never elated him; congratulations only bowed him in humility or caused a tear of joy to rise in his eyes. If in this book he has found it necessary to write of himself, he has had regard to what loyalty to the facts of the case called for, without the remotest wish to claim any credit for himself.

The blessing of God be upon all those into whose hands this book may come.

WM. W. LANDRUM.

*Richmond, Va., March 26th, 1895.*

# LIST OF PLATES.

Frontispiece, President Charles H. Corey.
Lumpkin's Jail.................................................. 47
First African Baptist Church............................. 61
Graduating Class, 1892...................................... 85
Richmond Theological Seminary......................... 89
Graduating Class, 1893...................................... 109
Rev James H. Holmes........................................ 133
Joseph Endom Jones, D. D................................. 157
David Nathaniel Vassar, D. D............................ 181
George Rice Hovey, A. M................................... 205

# HISTORY

OF

# RICHMOND THEOLOGICAL SEMINARY.

## CHAPTER I.

*Some Matters Personal—The United States Christian Commission—Schools for Colored Soldiers at Port Hudson—Getting out of the Red River.*

IT may not be unpardonable to make some references to the years the writer passed before commencing work in the South. The statements must be brief without any filling in of detail. Brought up in one of the back settlements of Canada, I did not know what a newspaper was until I was fourteen years of age. Being nearly a hundred miles from any city, and with no railroad communication, my opportunities for securing an education were but limited. I, however, succeeded in making due preparation, and entered Acadia College (now Acadia University), Nova Scotia, in 1854, and was graduated therefrom in 1858. Rev. E. A. Crawley, D. D., LL.D., when I entered, was president. He was a courtly gentleman, a ripe scholar and finished orator. Rev. J. M. Cramp, D. D., distinguished as a polemical and historical writer, was my teacher in Theology. In public and private life I heard much concerning Wilberforce, and the emancipation of the slaves in the West Indies. Dr. Crawley, who afterwards during the war was the teacher in a young ladies' seminary in South Carolina, oftentimes in my student days was grandly eloquent in his denunciations of the United States for holding so many millions in bondage. From these teachers of strong English type, who were familiar with the efforts of England in the work of emancipation, I was led to sympathize with those in bondage, and was prepared in a measure for what came to be my life work. From Prof. A. P. S. Stuart, a rare instructor, and from Rev. A. W. Sawyer, D. D., LL.D., the present efficient and beloved President of the University, was received a fondness for intellectual and literary work which has not left me during the excitement and activities of five and thirty years of public life.

During the spring of 1861, in the last year of my course at Newton Theological Institution, which I entered in 1858, were heard the rumblings, which were the forerunners of the oncoming storm of war. In July, 1861, a few days after being graduated from Newton Theological Institution, I became pastor of the First Baptist Church, Seabrook, N. H., where I remained until 1864.

The war came on. All over the land was heard

the tramp of marshalling armies. In front of the church where I preached young men were drilling. News was flashed across the wires of bloody battles, now victory, now defeat. Members of my own congregation were among the slain. Several trips were made to the front to look after these and after other soldiers. An organization known as the United States Christian Commission had been formed. Its delegates were to assist in looking after the dying on battle-fields, to carry comfort to thes ick and wounded in the hospitals, and to communicate with the friends of sick or dead soldiers.

Stirred by the exciting events of the hour, on the first of January, 1864, I gave up the charge of my church, and entered permanently into the service of the United States Christian Commission. My point of destination was New Orleans. Thence I pushed on to "the front" at Indianola, Texas. When the troops withdrew from that place, I followed them up the Rio Grande to Brownsville. When our work was done there, after a brief visit to Matamoras, Mexico, I returned to New Orleans, and was ordered to Port Hudson, on the Mississippi, where I first came in contact with educational workers among the colored people. With a letter of introduction from Chaplain T. M. Conway to Rev. E. S. Wheeler (now of Boston), Chaplain of the Eighth Regiment Corps d'Afrique, and to Lieutenant R. G. Seymour (now the Rev. R. G. Seymour, D. D., of Lowell, Mass.), I arrived at Port Hudson in April, 1864.

At this place systematic work had been commenced for the education of the large number of colored soldiers stationed at the Post. Captain Pease was in charge of the work of instruction of the Corps d'Afrique. Chaplain Wheeler, of the 80th United States Colored Infantry, had built in January, 1864, a school-house. Lieutenant R. G. Seymour, of the 79th Regiment of United States Colored Infantry, built a school-house for his regiment which was dedicated February 6th, 1864. It is recorded in Chaplain Wheeler's private diary, April 10th, 1864: "Brother C. H. Corey, of the Christian Commission, preached in the camp of the 3d Massachusetts Cavalry, and visited the School." Associated with Mr. Wheeler and Captain Pease in loyal service for the country, and incidentally in behalf of those colored veterans, were some well-known ministers of the Baptist denomination—Dr. Chase, of Philadelphia; Dr. Seymour, of Lowell, and Dr. Brouner, of New York.

Chaplain Wheeler, from whose report to Captain Pease I am courteously permitted to quote, under date of March 31st, 1864, says: "I am most heartily pleased with the earnestness and spirit of the men in overcoming the ignorance to which they have been subjected." In a report to Brigadier-General L. Thomas, he states that "the Orderly Sergeants, who four months ago were unable to distinguish an alphabetical character, are now able to transact considerable company business, having learned to read and write well." Captain Pease, Corps Instructor, testified to the enthusiasm and success with which the soldiers pursued their studies, and stated to me that they took as readily to books and to military tactics as the white soldiers. Dr. Wheeler, in a recent letter respecting the Schoolhouse above referred to, says: " I procured an order from our Division Commander, General Daniel Ullman, permitting me to tear down an old cotton-gin building outside of the fortifications, and erect it in a modified form in the rear of my tent, and there the men were not only instructed in a common school way, but religious services were usually held in it, by both officers and men." * * "Many of those colored soldiers made astonishing progress while under our care, eliciting most thoroughly the praise of their superior officers." He continues:

"The Hon. Orren McFadden, who finally became Lieutenant-Colonel of our Regiment, and who now resides in Cedar Grove, Maine, would join me, I am sure, in the warmest commendations of those men, whom he often referred to, in my presence, as 'exhibiting the most consummate bravery, manliness, and intelligence.'"

My visit to Port Hudson made impressions respecting this work which were never removed.

While at Port Hudson news came of defeat and repulse up the Red River. General Banks had fallen back, and in consequence of falling water some of his gunboats could not get below Alexandria. On arriving at this city I found thousands of men. Here was a fine field for Christian activity. Preaching, prayer-meetings, personal interviews with soldiers, white and colored, hospital service, and so on, absorbed all of my energies.

Finally the enemy got below us, cut off our communications, destroyed some of our transports, and planted batteries on the river banks. From two to three thousand men, for ten or twelve days and nights, worked under the leadership of Lieutenant-Colonel Joseph Bailey,* of the 4th Wisconsin Volunteers, " often up to their waists, and even to their necks in the water," until a dam was thrown partly across the river, which was 758 feet wide above Alexandria. By this means a sluice-way was formed. Our situation was growing desperate; our sick were increasing, and we were on short rations; our gunboats were unable to move, and the entire force was imperilled. The dam was fortunately a success. On a beautiful summer evening the gunboats swung from their moorings, and passed successfully through the sluice-way, to the delight of cheering thousands who stood beholding that thrilling spectacle. Next morning I strolled along the river bank which was

---

\* For the valuable services rendered to the fleet in this hour of great danger, this officer was promoted to the rank of Brigadier-General, and received the thanks of Congress. See " The Gulf and Inland Waters," by Commander Mahan of U. S. Navy.

lined with negro women and children; bales of cotton were thrown down the steep embankment and destroyed; the street was filled with moving army wagons. Presently a huge black smoke was observed rolling heavily upward.

The city was soon wrapped in flames; houses, stores, churches, everything seemed on fire; women and children were in tears, and the transports blew their whistles. I hastened through crowded streets, dodging among teams and infantry and galloping couriers, just in time to reach the Chauteau, the hospital boat to which I had been assigned, before she steamed out of danger. The fire was of incendiary origin, and General Banks sent men to extinguish it. The land forces had marched early in the day. Towards evening the fleet, consisting of about fifty vessels, including gunboats and transports, moved slowly down the river, until we tied up for the night. In the morning the infantry tried to cut its way across the country, a cloud of dust marking the line they took. The fleet moved cautiously down the river. The silence of those wooded shores was repeatedly broken by volleys poured into us by those concealed by earthworks on the bank. We finally reached Atchafalaya Bayou which the army crossed over, and we on the transports eventually reached New Orleans in safety.

## CHAPTER II.

*Morris Island—Entry into Charleston—Incidents—A Sunrise Prayer-Meeting—The First Sermon—The Dead Officer—The Disgusted Officer—A Mock Auction—Incidents—The Old Flag Back—Resolutions—Departure.*

A Summer in New England and the Maritime Provinces recruited exhausted energies and restored shattered health.

The late Nathan Bishop, LL.D., of honored memory, had charge of the New York branch of the United States Christian Commission, and under his supervision I was sent to the Department of the South, and made my headquarters before Charleston, on Morris Island. Here was spent the fall of 1864, and the early part of 1865. Distributing reading matter to the fleet and preaching to the soldiers, many of whom were colored, occupied my time. It was here that the siege of Charleston had been commenced on the 21st of August, 1863, by the opening of the "Swamp Angel" Battery. It was here on the 7th of September following that the gallant and lamented Shaw, Colonel of the 54th Massachusetts colored troops, fell at the capture of Fort Wagner.

The Confederates refused to give up his body. He lies there buried beside his brave soldiers who followed him to death and glory, " having won an immortal name, no less as the commander of the first negro regiment sent to the war, than by his gentle bearing as a man and bravery as a soldier." The following concerning Colonel Shaw is taken from A. D. Mayo, D. D., in his " New Education in the New South : "

"Years ago one of the bravest of the young commanders in the national army, Colonel Shaw, of the city of New York, fell, at the head of his brigade of colored soldiers, in a desperate assault on Fort Wagner, during the siege of Charleston. He was buried with his men, and his body was never found. After the close of the war the families, in New York and Boston, connected with the fallen soldier, built a school-house in Charleston for colored children, established the Shaw School and for several years supported it as a private beneficence. Some years since the building was virtually given to the city, and all the funds of the corporation passed over for its enlargement; and now one of the public Schools of Charleston bears the name of the New York colonel who died, at the head of his black brigade, forcing the entrance to that beleaguered city. \* \* \* \* \* \*

" My last visit was to the Shaw School, now a collection of several hundred children, with white and colored teachers; the principal, like the city superintendent, an officer in the Confederate army. I was invited to the great hall to listen to some exercises by the higher classes, prepared, as I understood, for their coming commencement exhibition. The first was a recitation, by a hundred of the older pupils, from Longfellow's " Building of the Ship: "

> 'Sail on, O Ship of State!
> Sail on, O Union, strong and great
> Humanity with all its fears,
> With all its hopes of future years,
> Is hanging breathless on thy fate!
> Our hearts, our hopes, are all with thee,
> Our hearts, our hopes, our prayers, our tears,
> Our faith triumphant o'er our fears,
> Are all with thee,—are all with thee!'

"Then, a boy as black as night, George Washington by name, was summoned from his seat to recite a pathetic poem, "The Dying Soldier." It didn't need comment to show for what cause that soldier died; for the poem was a most touching story of peril and suffering, even unto death, for the saving of the Union. As the soldier neared his end, he called to his companions for one more of the old songs of the village Sunday-school; and the whole body of children took up the theme and sung, with a pathos only heard in the tones of the freedmen, the dying refrain. The soldier breathed his last with a prayer for his country; when the entire crowd sprang to their feet and, led by their teachers, pealed forth—

'The Star Spangled Banner, O long may it wave
  O'er the land of free and the home of the brave!'"

The winter on Morris Island was spent without much excitement. There was an occasional false alarm; several blockade runners were captured, and shells were frequently thrown into the city. Occasionally a bullet from Fort Sumter, seven hundred yards away, would come whistling past the ear of some unsuspecting civilian or soldier who ventured upon the parapet of Fort Wagner. One soldier was hit at that distance away, and died from his wounds.

Fort Wagner was taken on the 7th of September, 1863, and for about fourteen months a slow bombardment continued from day to day until about thirteen thousand shells had been thrown into the town, or about one thousand per month. In the month of December, 1864, Savannah had fallen, through Sherman's famous march to the sea. Finally Sherman flanked Orangeburg, South Carolina, and General Hardee, who was in command at Charleston, was compelled to evacuate the place. General Hardee remained in the city until Friday night the 17th of February, leaving behind a detachment of cavalry to destroy what stores he could not remove. Colonel Bennett, commanding the Twenty-First Regiment United States colored troops on Morris Island, on Saturday morning, February 18th, 1865, hastened up the harbor in boats, and landed at

South Atlantic wharf. A detachment of the Fifty-Fourth Massachusetts Regiment followed. Some of these colored soldiers had been slaves in this very city. Now, with the old flag above them, they marched up the grass grown streets, past the slave marts, where their families and themselves had been sold in the public shambles, and laid aside their arms and helped extinguish the flames of the burning city. The following extracts from a letter which was written on the night of the day we entered the city will give some idea of the impression made on that occasion:

"All last night our gunboats kept up a continuous bombardment. The air was filled with bursting shells, and the sky was red with flame. This morning calm and beautiful heavy clouds of smoke rose in the direction of the city. The blowing up of heavy guns and gunboats sent echoes thundering from island to island. Orders came to pack and go to Charleston. The sand hills on Morris Island were lined with spectators. The sick and the lame had hobbled out from the hospitals, and in the still morning air stood looking at the dense clouds of smoke hanging over the city. I had been childish with joy all the morning. When I landed, scenes of indescribable desolation were all around me. In the lower half of the city (Gilmore's town as it was called) stores were open, private papers were blown about the streets, houses were shattered and roofless, streets ploughed up by the bursting shells, and steeples riddled. Pale, poorly clad and hungry people were on the streets. They received us with joy. Men, white as well as black, would come to me and grasp my hand. Sometimes with quivering lips and tearful eyes they would turn away without a word; their hearts were too full for utterance. When we entered the city flour was $1,600 per barrel. A man told me he had paid $200 for five pounds of sugar. A little boy told me that his shoes cost him $400. When a detachment of the Fifty-Fourth Massachusetts Regiment (colored) came along, the scenes I witnessed transcend human powers of description. It was the first body of colored men in arms seen in this city. The boys ran, and old men laughed and cried for joy; hats were swung, aprons and handkerchiefs waved. I saw young women dancing, the older ones shouting and praising God. I stood and wept; so did many a rough soldier; so did some of the citizens of Charleston. The negroes shook hands, and clung to the soldiers and seemed almost wild with delight."

This was in strange contrast with the scenes which had taken place in this city when Major Anderson, the peaceful Ordnance Sergeant in charge in Charleston harbor, was forced to surrender Fort Sumter, April 14, 1861. Then men and women were on the house-tops in the city, and gathered in the church steeples, bells were rung, guns fired, ladies waved their handkerchiefs. At night bonfires glowed; crowds surged through the streets, and there was hilarity and carousing, because, as Governor Pickens said, "the Stars and Stripes have been lowered in humility before the glorious little State of South Carolina?"\*

That night I found quarters in the west end of the Citadel Building, in one of the very rooms in which secession had been fostered. There the soldiers held a prayer meeting, which can never be forgotten. We had come over from Morris Island, rested and fresh without let or hindrance, and realizing that the war must soon end, there were prayers and thanksgiving such as are seldom heard. I quote from the following letter, written February 20th, 1865: "A happier day I never spent. I could not sleep; the scenes I had witnessed, the words I had heard, were still before me, and the anticipations of the coming Sabbath rendered it next to impossible to get any rest." Early I was away to a sunrise prayer-meeting among the colored people. I was the only white man present. I cannot describe the prayers and praise there offered. Said one, "*Who* could not praise the Lord this morning, who *would* not praise the Lord to-day, who would not praise *the Lord* that we can worship Him under our own vine and fig tree, and none shall make us afraid?" After the benediction they crowded around me in scores, all eager to grasp my hand; they got their hands around me, and even about

---

\* See Coffin's "Four Years of Fighting," p. 457.

my neck. Old wrinkled, toothless, ragged women came weeping, and pressed through the crowd to take my hand. Some got on the pulpit stairs and shouted "Hallelujah;" some got on the seats and stood weeping, looking over to where they crowded around me. I saw men embrace each other, and women, clasping hands, wept and laughed by turns.

Said one to me by way of apology, "Excuse us; this is a happy day for us." Some of the brethren made three attempts before they got me out of this throng; there were some hundreds present. One old man I saw weeping; he stood uttering, with intonations I cannot describe, "*Come at last*, come at *last*, come at last."

" Similar expressions I heard on every hand. At 10 A. M. I went out to find a Baptist meeting. All the white congregations of our denomination are scattered and the ministers are fled. So with the Methodists. I went to a group of colored people who had been to a Baptist meeting. They were congratulating each other. 'This is the most glorious day that Charleston has ever seen,' said one; another, 'I shed more tears yesterday than I ever did before;' another, 'I could not speak to a man yesterday without weeping.' In fine, wherever I went all seemed joyousness and sunshine. The children were full of glee; the old ones were almost frantic in their demonstrations, and the religious were filled with devout thanksgivings. In the afternoon I preached, according to appointment, in the spacious church where our morning service was held. I preached to more than 1500 people, black and white, citizens and soldiers, from Nehemiah xii, 43, 'The joy of Jerusalem was heard even afar off.' This was the first sermon preached in the city after its surrender. I never spoke to a more attentive congregation. When I prayed for the President of the United States there went up from nearly 2000 human beings such an 'Amen' as I never heard before. But how can I describe all. Your imagination may aid you to fill in the blank, when you think that these distressed thousands, hungry and naked, as many of them were, at the advent of the United States forces, were ushered at once into safety and freedom. The circumstances were unique, and those present on that occasion will not readily forget it."

My duties as Delegate of the United States Christian Commission, were to preach the gospel, to distribute religious reading matter, and to render such other services to the soldiers as might be needed. There were many interesting incidents told by soldiers, some of whom had been in prison and had made their escape. I remember a young soldier who came into my office, clothed in a suit of gray. He had made his escape from prison, and travelled by night, and remained concealed by day. At one time an old colored woman kept him hid for three weeks under the floor of her cabin. She killed the last pig that she owned, and purchased the suit of gray with the proceeds in order that the young man, by means of it, might escape. There were Union officers in prison in Charleston, some of whom, from time to time, made their escape. They concealed themselves in the deserted mansions in the shelled portions of the city. There was an interesting old man left in charge of one of these mansions by his master. He took in one of these escaping officers and concealed and cared for him. The officer was stricken down with yellow fever. Finally the guards came to search the premises for escaped prisoners. When the old man heard that they were approaching, he caught up the sick man, carried him up three pairs of stairs and concealed him under the roof. There he and another colored man cared for him three weeks, until he died. There was no other alternative but to dig a grave under the house and to bury him there. One day we crawled under the house and they showed me his grave. On the following fall I assisted the proper authorities in exhuming the body. We buried him in Magnolia Cemetery.

The remains of this officer, Lieutenant Reed, of an Ohio Regiment, were subsequently transferred to the National Cemetery at Hilton Head. There were several instances in which we disinterred the bodies of escaping officers, who had been cared for by the colored people, and who, becoming sick, had died and were buried in the yards of deserted houses.

As an illustration that predjudice existed even among some of the officers of the Union army, I will give an incident. One day a lieutenant of a Western regiment came into our reading-room. I noticed that his straps were not on his shoulders. He threw them down upon the counter with vehemence, exclaiming, " I will never wear those straps again, for I have seen a negro who outranks me." He had seen on the streets of Charleston, Dr. DeLaney, a very black man, who, by virtue of his position as Surgeon, ranked as Major, and who, of course, as an officer, was his superior. I did not then think that I should live to see the time when there would be more than 800 colored physicians in the United States.

During the month of March the colored people held a Jubilee celebration in which about 5,000 participated. I remember among other things a cart containing an auction block, with negroes for sale. The mock auctioneers had many bids, some as high as $15,000. An old woman ran screaming after the cart, feigning lamentations for her unfortunate " Chil'en." One old woman said as we passed by: " Mine all gone—sold in State Street—not one left to close my eyes." There was sadness in her tone and tears in her eyes. There were in the procession light-skinned and beautiful girls, with fair and flowing hair, linked hand in hand with black and curly headed ones, moving on in loving companionship with the rejoicing multitude.

It is not surprising that there were strong feelings and forceful expressions of the same among the people of Charleston, concerning the people of the North. An old gentleman, belonging to one of the old families of Charleston, was accustomed to frequent our rooms to read the papers always kept on file. One day, in explaining the reason of the excessive heat, he said it was "because there were so many emissaries from Hell in Charleston." On being asked to whom he referred, he replied, "Why, you—you—;" he saw his dilemma, and the sentence remained unfinished.

My office was next to the Charleston Hotel. On returning from service one night, I heard a great commotion. Officers were shouting; some were standing on the counter, some singing, some crying for joy; others were hugging each other, and some astride the necks of others. I asked, "What is the matter? What does all this mean?" Said they, "Have you not heard the news? Lee has surrendered." There were cheers, songs and rejoicings until a late hour.

The following letter written a few weeks later, April 17th, after I had seen the same flag, which was shot from its staff in 1861, restored to its place, by the gallant defender who was in command when Sumter fell. I leave it to the reader's imagination to contrast the changed conditions and relations of the people of Charleston on these two ever memorable occasions:

"Last Friday was a great day here. Hundreds of visitors were on from the North. The city was alive with excitement. At 10 A. M. the steamers were in readiness to take us to Fort Sumter. Seats and decorations had been prepared, and hundreds of army and navy officers with invited guests were anxiously awaiting the appearance of the orator, Rev. Henry Ward Beecher. At last he came. Prayer was offered accompanied by the *Amens* of thousands. Mr. Beecher delivered an impassioned and eloquent oration. The "old flag," which was lowered four years ago, was then taken from its hiding place and attached to the rope. Major-General Anderson delivered a brief and impressive address. The tears were rolling down the old hero's cheeks. He then proceeded to raise the flag to its place. Such a scene I never expect to witness again. Every heart was moved. I think that there was scarcely a person who did not weep. Then the air was rent with cheers, and the cannon boomed. Every fort that fired on Fort Sumter four years ago saluted the flag, as did all the vessels in the harbor.

I stood on the parapet and witnessed the whole, with emotions not to be described. What increased the depth of the feeling manifested by all was the reception that morning of the news that Lee and his army had surrendered. The next day there was a large meeting which called out thousands of whites and blacks. George Thompson, of England;

Judge Kelly, of Pennsylvania; Theodore Tilton, and William Lloyd Garrison, the great Abolitionist, were among the speakers. Such a meeting I have never seen and can never see again, for the circumstances can never occur again. All who spoke gave all the glory to God. After the meeting, the colored children singing " John Brown's Body Lies a Mouldering," with waving of handkerchiefs escorted the speakers to the Charleston Hotel. Henry Ward Beecher preached on Sunday to three or four thousand people. Only think, Garrison, Beecher, Thompson, and Tilton speaking here in this city. What changes four years have wrought."

As I was about to leave Charleston, the following, which explains itself, was placed in my hands:

WENTWORTH ST. BAPTIST CHURCH, *May 14th, 1865.*

At a meeting of the members of this church and congregation, held this day after morning service, Mr. W. N. Hughes was called to the chair, and Mr. W. J. Heriot appointed Secretary. The following preamble and resolutions, offered by Deacon W. B. Heriot, were unanimously adopted:

*Whereas*, the Rev. Charles H. Corey, agent of the United States Christian Commission has, for several months past, taken charge of the Baptist Church in Wentworth Street, in the city of Charleston, during which time he has, without pecuniary compensation, regularly maintained public worship therein on each successive Sabbath, and having, by the courteousness of his demeanor, the usefulness of his instructions, the exemplariness of his character, and the interest he has manifested in the welfare of our church, most justly entitled himself to our high esteem and deep gratitude; and whereas, Mr. Corey has informed us that his appointed duties will in future prevent him from continuing to perform services at our church; therefore we, the members of the church and congregation, who have enjoyed the privilege of Mr. Corey's acquaintance and Christian ministry, deem it a duty we owe to ourselves to give expression to our feelings on this occasion. And to that intent we do unanimously resolve as follows:

1. That our heartfelt thanks are justly due and are hereby cordially tendered to the Rev. Charles H. Corey, for the ministerial services he has so cheerfully and acceptably performed in our church during the past few months.

2. That we have learned with regret that the appointed duties of Mr. Corey will hereafter prevent him from continuing his services at our church; and that the best wishes and prayers are, that he may continue in health and be abundantly prospered in the good work in which he is so faithfully engaged, wherever, in the providence of God, his lot may be cast.

3. That a copy of this preamble and resolutions be transmitted to Mr. Corey over the signatures of the Chairman and Secretary of this meeting.

W. N. HUGHES, Chairman.
W. J. HERIOT, Secretary.

After closing up all the offices of the United States Christian Commission in the Department of the South our footsteps were turned homeward. Arrangements completed, our noble steamer swung away from the dock at Hilton Head, the point of departure of government steamers, amid the cheers of hundreds of war-worn veterans, who now flushed with victory, after four years of absence, were returning to quiet homes nestling among New Enggland hills or dotting western prairies. The soldiers sang their old camp songs, and the dear old hymns sung around the fireside at home. There were teachers returning to rest awhile from their toils; and sailors, and soldiers, and preachers, and Christian Commission men, all of whom mingled in delightful converse.

At night the stars from their silent thrones smiled serenely upon a grateful and happy throng. Many had been anxious to take some trophy from the field, a remembrance of the camp-fire, or a keepsake from the sunny clime. So there were mocking birds, guinea pigs, poodles, kittens, turtles and snakes on board. Finally, New York was approached. How gracefully the clouds sailed along the morning sky, and cast their shadows on the distant shores! How grateful after the dangers and excitements of the field was the perfume stealing over the waters on the invigorating breezes from the distant clover fields! How pleasant to be far from the hoarse discords of war and the carnage of the battle-field! Our eyes were no longer to look upon the windrows of the slain, nor upon streams and harbors crimsoned with fraternal blood. The angel of peace had spread her white wings over mountains and valleys, and joy and gladness filled all the land.

## CHAPTER III.

*Missionary Work in South Carolina—Condition of the Churches—Church Organized in the Woods—On the Sea Islands—Rev. T. Willard Lewis and other Methodist Workers—Statistics—The Augusta Institute.*

DURING the spring of 1865, Rev. Dr. Lathrop and J. W. Hoyt visited Charleston, and seeing the wide field of usefulness that was presented among the colored people urged me to continue in the South, and to commence labor among them. Accordingly, in the autumn of 1865, my wife and I sailed for Charleston, South Carolina. Here I commenced my labors under the auspices of the American Baptist Home Mission Society. In addition to preaching in the city, where I assisted in organizing churches, I made trips to the interior of the State establishing churches and ordaining ministers. Rev. James Hamilton, a colored brother from Philadelphia, and others assisted me in some of these services. The colored members in most instances belonged to the white churches. In some places, however, there was not a single white member of a church among the whites to be found. At Georgetown there was only one, the clerk, and he lived fourteen miles out of town. Churches were organized and ministers ordained in all the important cities and villages of the State. At Camden, Rev. Mr. Boykin was ordained. One of his sons, at that time unborn, has since grown to manhood, and taken his degree of Bachelor of Divinity at the Richmond Theological Seminary. At Chester a church was organized.

It was also desirable to establish a church in an outlying community. The brethren were fearful of violence in those unsettled times, and determined upon a journey by night as the only possible course to pursue. Accordingly we started at nine o'clock and travelled nearly twenty miles, some on horseback and some in wagons, in the wintry night. On Sunday morning, around an open fire in the woods, we organized the Pilgrim Baptist Church, and ordained Rev. Sancho Sanders as its pastor. We returned to our starting place, passing through Chester on Sunday night in the darkness. Trips were made on foot, on horseback, by steamers, and in row boats. Along the railroads it was no uncommon thing to see the railroad rails bent and twisted in the form of U. S., showing that Uncle Sam had put his mark upon the places through which his armies had marched. Visits were made to Edisto, Wadmelaw and James Islands, and churches were established. Oftentimes a number of brethren accompanied me. We rowed for many miles, and the weird songs of the boatmen, with bared head, feet and arms, floated far over the calm waters. From a number of churches established at this time students for the ministry have come to the school at Richmond. A number of faithful and devoted men, who were placed in charge of these churches, have gone to their reward. Some of them were eminently holy and consecrated, and the influence of their lives and ministry is still felt among the churches of the State. Others still survive, and are the veteran leaders in all denominational enterprises.

I cannot speak of those days of pioneer work without referring to the energetic and beloved Rev. T. Willard Lewis and his devoted wife. In their family I found a pleasant home. We often journeyed together along dangerous and unfrequented roads. He was caring for his Methodist brethren, and I for the Baptists. He founded the Baker Institute, which eventually became Clafflin University. He fell at his post, years ago, a victim to yellow fever. His wife also has gone to her reward. So has Dr. A. Webster, the associate and successor of brother Lewis. His house was also our home for a while. His wife, too, has passed away. There were strong ties that bound our hearts together in those days of anxiety and oftentimes of danger.

Nor can I forget the youthful and devoted Randolph, a colored missionary of the Methodist Episcopal Church, who, for a time, recited Hebrew to me, and who was deliberately assassinated on a railroad platform in the country, while waiting for his train. These noble men and women, after living honored and useful lives, rest from their labors, and their works do follow them.

In the spring of 1867 a Convention of the colored Baptists of the State was called. Delegates from nearly a dozen churches met in the Morris Street Church on May 1st. Rev. I. P. Brockenton was the President, and J. C. Pawley the Secretary.

Out of this Convention grew the Gethsemane Association, the first in the State. There are now in the State twenty-eight associations, 764 churches, 444 ministers, and more than 120,000 members. Rev. Jacob Legare (pronounced La-grée), a man of pure life and of deep spirituality, was the beloved pastor of the Morris Street Baptist Church. He was highly esteemed by the late Dr. E. T. Winkler, white pastor in Charleston. Rev. Mr. Legare died lamented by all, and left no stain upon his memory. My relations to all the pastors and the churches were of the pleasantest kind, and I look back to those pioneer days of missionary life as among the happiest of my life. Several of the pastors and many of the young men of the State have since been students in the Seminary at Richmond.

In the spring of 1867 I closed my missionary work in South Carolina, and in the autumn of that year I went to Augusta, Georgia, under the auspices of the National Theological Institute and University, and here commenced educational work as President of the Augusta Institute. The times, politically, were unsettled. Prejudices were strong, and with but few facilities, not very much was accomplished. A few came to me for instruction by day, and a larger class at night. Sermons were preached, and some churches were organized. I left Augusta on the 13th of July, 1868, and was subsequently transferred to another field, Richmond, Virginia, and Rev. Lucius E. Hayden, D. D., became my immediate successor as President of the Augusta Institute.

In a Historical Sketch of the *Augusta Institute* by J. T. Robert, LL.D., the following statement concerning the work done during this period may be found:

"In November of the same year (1867), Rev. Charles H. Corey and wife commenced their labors here, retaining the services of Mr. Rice.

"Mr. Corey, in his first quarterly report, February 1, 1868, gives thirty-eight pupils in attendance; seventeen in theological class, fifteen in young men's and six in Mrs. Corey's. In his second report, April 18, 1868, sixty were in attendance, seventeen of whom were ministerial students. The school was kept in a rented room,* and mostly at

---

* Dr. Robert is slightly in error here. We met in the Springfield (colored) Baptist Church. I may say that, in addition to teaching, I preached every Sunday. These were times of great political excitement, but no harm befell me. I had some warnings from the Ku Klux Klan, and on a few occasions the city authorities, unsolicited by me, sent some policemen to protect our evening school. Rev. Dr. Cuthbert, the pastor of the white Baptist church, gave me his sympathy and cordial support, and remained my friend until his death.

night; so that Mr. Corey did not return to his lodgings generally 'till about midnight. The branches taught were as diversified as the wants of those who attended it. The Institute had warm friends in the community. God's blessing was with it. But buildings were needed for its use, and also funds to aid pupils from abroad in their support. Mr. Corey's labors in Augusta closed July 13th, 1868, and he was subsequently transferred to the Richmond Institute, Virginia, to meet an exigency which the resignation of teachers had created there."

## CHAPTER IV.

*The Evacuation of Richmond—The Burning of the city—Mr. Lumpkin's Coffle of Slaves—Lecture by Dr. Burrows—President Lincoln in Richmond—Lumpkin's Jail—His Daughters in a Northern Seminary—Rev. Mr. Newman's Experience.*

IT may not be out of place to introduce here a brief statement of the exciting events which occurred at the Evacuation of Richmond. For the most of my information I am indebted to Charles Carleton Coffin, who, in his "Four years of Fighting," gives an account of what he learned and what he saw on entering the burning city. Mr. Coffin was the war correspondent ("Carleton") of the Boston *Journal* during the years of the war.

On Sunday April 2d, 1865, a messenger brought a dispatch from General Lee to Jefferson Davis, who was found in Dr. Minnigerode's church, which read, "My line is broken in three places and Richmond must be evacuated." Mr. Davis repaired to his office and wrote an order for the evacuation of the city. All was commotion, and preparations for speedy departure were made on every hand. Mr. Lumpkin, the keeper of a slave trader's jail, made up a coffle of fifty men, women and children in his jail yard, "within pistol shot of Jeff. Davis's parlor window and a stone's throw from the Monumental church," and hurried them to the Danville Depot. "This sad and weeping fifty, in handcuffs and chains, was the last slave coffle that shall tread the soil of America."\* On that Sunday afternoon, when Jefferson Davis, his Secretaries, Benjamin and Trenholm, when Dr. Hoge and Dr. Duncan, when the whole Confederate Government was on the move, "coaches, carriages, wagons, carts, wheelbarrows, and everything in the shape of a vehicle was pressed into use." All were hastening to get away from the doomed city. "There was a jumble of boxes, chests, trunks, valises, carpet-bags, a crowd of excited men, sweating as never before, women with dishevelled hair, unmindful of their wardrobes, wringing their hands, children crying in the crowd, sentinels guarding each entrance to the train, pushing back, at the point of the bayonet, the panic-stricken multitude." But there was no room for Mr. Lumpkin and his slaves.

Early on the following morning, after the departing of the Confederate troops, the city was set on fire by order of the Confederate General Ewell. The last division has crossed the river. "The sun is up. A match is applied to the turpentine that has been poured over the timbers" of the bridges leading to Manchester, and they are in flames; so too the tobacco warehouses, the flouring mills, the arsenals,

---

\* See Coffin's "Four Years of Fighting," p. 501-5.

the laboratory, and whole blocks of the business portion of the city, until thirty squares in all are swept by the flames, and many millions of dollars worth of property are destroyed.* As the fire rages, General Weitzel enters the city, the colored soldiers singing the John Brown song. They pass through streets flanked with flame to the Capitol. They stack their guns and lay aside their knapsacks; they spring to the engines; they mount the roofs; they tear down burning buildings, and seek to stay the ravages of the fires kindled by the departing soldiers. The Capitol square is filled with furniture, beds, clothing, crockery, chairs, tables, and looking-glasses. Women are weeping, children crying. Men stand speechless, gazing at the desolation. The colored soldiers emulate the noble example of their comrades in arms in Charleston, and forgetting self in their devotion to duty, seek to save the homes and property of their former owners, and divide their rations with the houseless women and children.

Mr. Coffin, after continuing his graphic description, comments as follows: "How stirring the events of that day! Lee retreating, Grant pursuing; Davis a fugitive; the Governor and Legislature of Virginia seeking safety in a canal boat; Doctors of

---

*The value of public and private property destroyed some have placed as high as $10,000,000. The Richmond *Whig*, of April 12th, 1865, says: "It is remarkable that this fire swept away almost every vestige of the Confederate Government from our city." See Note B.

Divinity fleeing from the wrath they feared; the troops of the Union marching up the streets; the old flag waving over the Capitol; rebel ironclads blowing up; Richmond on fire; the billows rolling from square to square, unopposed in their progress by the bewildered crowd; and the Northern Vandals laying down their arms, not to the enemy in the field, but the better to battle with a foe not more relentless, but less controllable with the weapons of war. Weird the scenes of that strange, eventful night,—The glimmering flames; the clouds of smoke, hanging like a funeral pall above the ruins; the crowd of homeless creatures wandering in the streets."

It is well known that the Union forces on entering the city undertook to save the property of the citizens, and to restore confidence.

A writer in the Richmond *Whig* of April 7th, 1865, says: "With bland and open countenances and arms, the Union Army meets us like brothers. They pity our misfortunes. They have restored order to our city. They have saved us from anarchy. They desire to supply our wants, relieve the suffering, to bless and heal."

And a writer in the *Whig* again says, when 12,000 Union soldiers marched on review through the streets of Richmond: "They marched orderly and quietly, as though desirous of abstaining from any unnecessary demonstrations that might tend to give offence to citizens."

Dr. J. L. Burrows, for many years pastor of the First Baptist church in Richmond, in a brilliant and thrilling lecture on "The Fall of Richmond," speaks of the efforts of the United States soldiers to save the burning city, and graphically describes the march of a regiment of colored troops up Broad street. Along the sidewalk there were their parents, wives and sisters, some of whom they had not seen for years. But oblivious to the exclamations of joyful recognition, with heads erect and steady step, and with eyes to the front, on, on marched the regiment, " the very *perfection of discipline.*"

Mr. Coffin describes the walk of President Lincoln through the streets of Richmond, amid the wild huzzas of the excited and rejoicing multitudes, and details an incident.

" The walk from the landing to the Davis mansion was long, and the President halted a moment to rest. 'May de good Lawd bless you, President Linkum,' said an old negro, removing his hat and bowing with tears of joy rolling down his cheeks. The President removed his own hat, and bowed in silence; it was a bow which upset the forms, laws, customs and ceremonies of centuries of slavery. It was a death shock to chivalry and a mortal wound to caste."

Lumpkin's jail has been referred to. Perhaps it may be well, at this time, to give further particulars concerning this place. It was situated in " The Bottom" between Franklin and Broad Streets, on the west side of Shockoe Creek. It occupied a portion of the ground now covered by the establishment of Chamblin, Delancy & Scott. A narrow lane known as Wall Street, properly Fifteenth Street, led to it. This establishment, which has been often spoken of as the "old slave pen," consisted of four buildings, which were of brick. One

LUMPKIN'S JAIL.

was used by the proprietor as his residence and his office. Another was used as a boarding-house for the accommodation of those who came to sell their slaves or to buy. A third served as a bar-room and a kitchen. The "old jail" stood in a field a few rods from the other buildings. It was forty-one feet long and two stories in height, with a piazza to both stories on the north side of the building. Here men and women were lodged for safe-keeping, until they were disposed of at private or public sale. The proprietor had a family of interesting daughters, whom he sent North to be educated.

In the summer of 1891, I spent a Sunday in the home of Rev. Mr. Mower, of Kennebunkport, Maine. Conversation incidently turned upon matters pertaining to the past. Mrs. Mower, formerly Annie E. Cauldwell, knew Martha and Anna Lumpkin at Mrs. John C. Cowles' Female Seminary, at Ipswich, Massachusetts, when she was there as a little girl in 1856.

These girls, though born of a slave mother, were so white that they passed in the community as white ladies. The father, fearing that some financial contingency might arise when these, his own beautiful daughters, might be sold into slavery to pay his debts, kept them, after their education had been completed, in the free State of Pennsylvania, where they would be safe. I saw these daughters in Philadelphia, and found them to be cultivated and refined, and contented and happy with families of their own.

The following incident, given by Rev. A. M. Newman, of Opelousas, Louisiana, at the Special Meeting of the American Baptist Home Mission Society, held in Nashville, in 1888, gives us a picture of one kind of work carried on in the Lumpkin Establishment, and also furnishes an illustration of the truthfulness of the remark sometimes heard, that truth is oftentimes stranger than fiction. Brother Newman, the former neglected slave boy, after graduating at Madison University, became the influential pastor of large and important churches. I quote from his address, delivered on the occasion above referred to. The address may be found in the November number of the Baptist Home Mission Monthly, for 1888, page 295.

"Dr. Corey and Brother Holmes were talking last night about Richmond and Lumpkin's jail, and wondering at the change that had taken place. I thought of one of those changes that took place in my own individual history. About the year 1862, the person with whom I was living called me and said, 'Take this note and carry it down to Mr. Lumpkin.' Well I took the note, went off down Broad street just as happy as a little fellow could be. I handed Mr. Lumpkin the note, and as I passed I saw Mrs. Mary Jane Lumpkin, his colored wife, and noticed that she looked at me rather piteously. I could not understand it. I presented the note and Mr. Lumpkin looked at it and said: 'Here John, take this boy, carry him back there and put him in.' It seemed to me that my heart went right down. I could not understand it, but there may be some of my brothers here to-day who understand what it means by 'putting him in.' I was glad enough when I came out, and when I came away that same woman looked at me again, and it seemed to me that she was saying, 'poor child.' I went on back to the place where I was living.

Some brother asks what I mean by 'putting him in.' It was putting me in a place known as the whipping room, and on the floor of that room were rings. The individual would be laid down, his hands and feet stretched out and fastened in the rings, and a great big man would stand over him and flog him. I got out of there in 1862, and went home. Time passed on. By and by great things came to us. We were all free. Prison walls were broken down. As soon as possible I went to Wayland Seminary, D. C. From there I went to Madison University, and then, in 1873, to New Orleans to take charge of a church. One day while we were having a church meeting a splendid looking lady came down the aisle, and coming up to the pastor presented a very nice looking letter. I opened it and looked at it and read: 'To whom it may concern: This is to certify that Sister Mary Jane Lumpkin is a member in good and regular standing in the First African Baptist church, city of Richmond, and is hereby dismissed by her own free will and consent to join with you.' Then I looked up and said, 'Is this Sister Lumpkin?' She said, 'This is Sister Lumpkin,' and looked at me and said, 'Have I not seen you before?' I said, 'I expect you have.' She remarked, 'Are you not the little one that came one morning down to the jail with a note, and are you not the one that went into the back room?' 'Yes, I *am* the same one,' said I. '*Ah*,' she said. But brethren I will not tell you any more about it."

## CHAPTER V.

*Condition of the Freedmen at the close of the War—Work in their behalf by the American Baptist Home Mission Society—Early Work in Richmond—The National Theological Institute and University—Dr. N. Colver—Dr. Robert Ryland—Dr. Parker's Lectures—Resolutions.*

WHEN slavery was abolished in the District of Columbia, April 16th, 1862, and after the emancipation proclamation of January 1st, 1863, thousands of freedmen crowded into Washington, Alexandria and other places occupied by the Union army. Scantily clad and without means, they were fed and sheltered in shanties, sheds and slave-pens. These multitudes of dependent men, women and children, bewildered by their new surroundings, with no self-reliance, and without guides or counsellors, afforded an ample field for the labors of Christian men and women. And later, when the war had ended and four millions of homeless, penniless, friendless waifs, with no utensils, no lands, no churches, no schools, no business experience, were thrust forth into the heart of the nation, to compete with a dominant race, the situation was indeed appalling. Every Christian and every patriot recognized the importance of providing for them properly trained and qualified teachers and preachers.

As early as June 25th, 1862, the Executive Board of the American Baptist Home Mission Society had voted to occupy such Southern fields as the providence of God might open to them.

In September, 1863, the Society, which had sent some missionary workers into the South in 1862, adopted "a positive and pronounced policy" respecting the work for the colored people. Before April, 1864, they had about twenty missionaries and assistants in the Southern field. In 1865, the Board of the Home Mission Society was instructed to prosecute, "in all wise and feasible ways, the evangelization of the freedmen, and to aid them in the erection and procurement of church and school edifices when requisite." The tide of feeling, particularly in New England, ran very strong in this direction. Prominent men in the denomination offered themselves for the service. Operations were eventually commenced at various important centres in the South.

J. G. Binney, D. D., at one time President of the Columbian College, Washington, D. C., and subsequently teacher of a theological class at Rangoon, Burmah, opened in the city of Richmond, in the month of November, a school under the patronage of the American Baptist Home Mission Society, for the instruction of colored men preparing for the ministry. The *Religious Herald*, published at Richmond, in making announcement of this fact under the date of November 30th, 1865, says: "Dr. Binney's age, learning, experience, piety and prudence eminently fit him for the work in which he is engaged." Dr. Binney had a class of from twenty to twenty-five, whom he could hear only at night. "The effort to provide suitable accommodations for Rev. Dr. Binney's School failed," and he did not long remain in Richmond, but at an early day returned to Burmah and gave himself to the work of training a native ministry among the people of the far East, a work for which he was so eminently qualified. For many years after this, "he filled the post of President of the Karen Theological Seminary at Rangoon."

It becomes necessary at this point to make some statements concerning the NATIONAL THEOLOGICAL INSTITUTE AND UNIVERSITY.

An organization known as the "National Theological Institute," composed of prominent Baptists, was effected at Washington, D. C., in December, 1864, and commenced operations early in 1865. This Institution, which had for its object the judicious training of men of God for the Christian ministry, and of others associated with them as assistants, was chartered on the 10th of May, 1866. This charter was amended March 2d, 1867, and the name was changed to that of "The National Theological Institute and University." Of this organization J. D. Fulton, D. D., became President, and

J. W. Parker, D. D., Corresponding Secretary. He was succeeded as Secretary by Solomon Peck, D. D. J. W. Converse, of Boston, was the Treasurer. The work of the National Theological Institute and University was divided into two departments. First—Schools were established at important points, so that the more influential pastors of churches might be helped without removing them from their work and from their pastoral charges. Secondly—Ministers' Institutes were "organized in a manner similar to those which were first established in the West." By this means it was hoped to reach the masses of the ministry.

When this Society had entered fairly upon its work, attention was directed to Nathaniel Colver, D. D., as one eminently fitted, by his antecedents, by his sympathies, by his power as a Biblical teacher, and his tact in addressing and influencing men, for the service needed in the Department of Instruction. He received an invitation while Professor of Biblical Theology in the Theological Seminary, at Chicago, to enter the service of the National Institute. He accepted, and on May 13th, 1867, he arrived in Richmond and made arrangements to commence his work. July 1st, 1867, he leased, for three years, at one thousand dollars per annum, the establishment known as Lumpkin's Jail, which has been described already. It was in the Old Jail, the threshold of which was pressed by the foot of a slave for the last time on the memorable Sunday afternoon of the evacuation, that Dr. Colver made a beginning of his work. Appropriate services were held on the premises, and Dr. Colver preached an impressive sermon from the porch of the boarding-house. He referred to the change that had taken place in the status of the colored people, and also to the different purpose to which the premises were about to be devoted; to the old jail, with the iron grating across the windows (a place of bitter memories), that was in the adjacent yard. No longer would there go up from within those walls from broken-hearted men, torn from their families forever, an agonizing wail to Heaven. No longer would helpless wives and mothers wash those floors with their tears. The Doctor urged all ministers and young men to avail themselves of the opportunity to enter the School. The occasion was one of profound and tearful interest.

Dr. Colver made arrangements with Rev. James H. Holmes, pastor of the First African Baptist Church, to reside with his family on the premises, and to look after the establishment. School opened regularly in the fall of 1867, and Robert Ryland, D. D., was associated with Dr. Colver during the year.

Dr. Ryland was for twenty-eight years President of Richmond College; and for twenty-five years pastor of the First African Baptist Church. He says in the *Religious Herald* of September 12th, 1869: " For twenty-five years preceding the collapse of the Confederacy, I labored on the Sabbath and at other spare hours for the spiritual welfare of the colored people." Dr. Colver, seeing Dr. Ryland returning from the market with his basket on his arm, decided to secure his services as an associate in teaching. As an illustration of the great change which took place at the close of the war in the circumstances of the citizens, this distinguished leader and preacher, in order to support his family, carried milk around the city and sold it, alike to white and black. Dr. Ryland refers to this in a letter to the Richmond *Dispatch*, August 24th, 1876, in which he says: "I did not keep a dairy, but possessed one cow, whose milk, carried on foot to my customers, morning and evening, sustained my family for many months." Dr. Ryland was a man "pious, consistent and laborious," and his labors, which were continued through one year, closing with August 31st, 1868, were highly appreciated by the young men of the School. He speaks of the work as "A great and good one," and earnestly prays for a "large reward" upon his "fellow laborer in the cause of Christ." Dr. Ryland makes the following statement concerning the work done by him in the School:

"My connection with your Institute began about the 1st of September, 1867, and ended about the last of June, 1868. Dr. Colver, the Principal, taught only Biblical knowledge, and I devoted six full hours a day in teaching all the elementary branches that I saw most needful to the pupils. I got along very pleasantly with all the students, and with Dr. Colver. But as it was best for him to continue, and as a female could teach at $600 per annum, what I was teaching at a cost to the Society of $1,200, I suggested to Dr. Peck, who had come to Richmond partly to lecture to the School and partly to attend to its fiscal matters, that I ought to resign. He concurred with me, and I acted accordingly, with the kindest feelings toward the whole enterprise.

"Dr. Parker and Dr. Peck delivered some most judicious and valuable lectures to the whole School in the winter of 1867–68, on theological subjects. But as I was generally engaged with my classes when Dr. Colver was with his, I did not form an opinion of his instructions, that is, a very definite one." "The School began systematically about September 1st, 1867, in a building known as Lumpkin's Jail, with some thirty or forty pupils, two-thirds of whom had some reference to the ministry."

Concerning the course of lectures above referred to, Miss E. H. Peck, who was in the office of her father in Boston during his absence, says: "Dr. Parker was to assist Drs. Colver and Ryland in giving instruction. But Dr. Parker has been sick in Washington and Dr. Colver is very feeble, and often suffers from sudden and severe disease in his chest, threatening life; so my father has gone to the rescue, and writes that he arrived none too soon, and finds himself fully occupied with lecturing, teaching, receiving calls, etc."

Dr. Colver, in consequence of failing health, resigned in June, 1868. He died at Chicago, Illinois, September 25th, 1870. An account of the life and services of this distinguished man may be found in the valuable memoir prepared by Rev. J. A. Smith, D. D.

In accepting the resignations of Drs. Colver and Ryland as teachers at Richmond, the Executive Committee placed on record the following resolutions, adopted June 15th, 1868:

*Resolved*, That in accepting the resignation of the Rev. Dr. Ryland, we wish to express our deep sympathy with his Christian spirit, and our high admiration for his manly firmness and noble fidelity to truth and duty, which he has evinced in continuing amid all the changes which have occurred in the community around him, his life-long devotion to the interests of the colored people.

*Resolved*, That we recognize with grateful hearts the services which have been performed by Dr. Colver in the interests of the freedmen; that we feel devoutly thankful to God for the agent and agency; and that, while we accept his resignation as theological teacher at Richmond, Virginia, it is not without the hope that his valuable services may be secured in some other department of the grand educational enterprise to which his whole soul is so thoroughly committed.

To meet the exigency created by the above resignations, the Rev. Mr. Corey was subsequently transferred to Richmond from the Augusta Institute.

## CHAPTER VI.

*Dr. Colver's Work in Richmond—Letters—Transfer of the Work of the N. T. I. and U. to the American Baptist Home Mission Society—Report of Work done.*

IN carrying out the plan referred to in the last chapter, Mr. and Mrs. Corey repaired to Richmond, September 16th, 1868.

School was formally commenced October 1st, with Miss H. W. Goodman as chief assistant. Classes were opened on the night of the 21st for such as could not attend in the daytime. In November and December of this year, by order of the Executive Committee, a Ministers' Institute was held in connection with the School. Dr. J. W. Parker and the Principal were the lecturers. Eighty-one ministers and church officers, in addition to the regular students, attended this special Institute. At the close of the fall term more than one hundred had been regularly connected with the School, with an average daily attendance of sixty.

Dr. Parker reports to Dr. Peck in December, concerning this series of lectures, "The Lord is giving us favor here. In the day and evening courses together, I have had about one hundred men—every colored pastor in the city. The number increases every day. If we could continue until February 15th, we should be obliged to take the African Church and address five hundred. But it is better to wait. It is most inspiring work. The men are more eager than ever. Many of them are in tears much of the time, as we speak of doctrines and duties. I enjoy the work exceedingly. I have nightly to express my gratitude to God, with tears, for the privilege of lifting into light Christ's 'little ones' who sit in darkness."

Dr. Colver had been invited to aid in this Special Course of Instruction, but the state of his health would not warrant it.

Concerning the Ministers' Institutes which were held at Richmond and elsewhere with great success, from 1868–1869, Dr. J. W. Parker,* who conducted several in the South, under the auspices of the National Theological Institute and University, writes from Washington, D. C., April 26th, 1868, of those whom he had under his instruction at that time:

"Some had no more use of their reasoning powers than a blind man has of his eyes, and others had much power of thought, but had no breadth of foundation of knowledge of the Bible beyond the

---

* Dr. Parker was for more than twenty years pastor of a Baptist Church in Cambridge, Massachusetts. He also served as Secretary of the Northern Baptist Education Society, and subsequently became pastor of the Calvary Baptist Church, Washington, D. C.

FIRST AFRICAN BAPTIST CHURCH.

simplest elements of Christian truth. All were without any knowledge of the relation of the Old Testament to the New, or of the Gospels to the Epistles. * * * I think we give these men power with their people as we make them able to refer to the Scriptures for what they teach and direct. If we do little more for them than to help them to read and to refer to a few Scriptures which teach doctrine and duty, much is gained. It is not the amount of knowledge which we impart so much as the fullness of possession which they have of a few truths and their relations. If they can be held to the simple truths in doctrine and precept, they will lead the people more safely and successfully."

Dr. Parker again writes from Savannah, Georgia, March 20th, 1869: "This year opens the way for much more effective labor the next. If you ask me who will perform it, He knows who has liberated this people, and intends that they shall be taught, and I have no knowledge nor solicitude in the matter. My heart has been greatly enlarged in it, and I have much gratitude to God for the privilege of doing the little I have been permitted to do. It has absorbed my whole being and filled all my horizon. * * * I have been out of the world for three months, have seen but two numbers of the *Watchman*, know nothing of what is going on in the world or the Church, but I reckon the Lord will be able to manage without my supervision, and I am content to leave the matter with Him."

In order to understand the kind of work done at Richmond by Drs. Colver and Ryland, I will introduce a letter written to me while in charge of the Augusta Institute, Augusta, Georgia. I wrote Dr. Colver, asking him kindly to make such suggestions as his experience and observation would warrant. He writes from Richmond, Virginia, November 18th, 1867 :

"The enquiries you make will best be answered by your own observation of those who compose your pupils, and their necessities. The field is new and peculiar, and peculiar treatment is demanded. We almost have to make the mind to instruct. Of course our theological instructions must be dogmatical till we can teach them to reason, and till they can read and gather to themselves the use of terms. I have a large evening class of over thirty that I have to teach to speak and read properly; and some in figures and writing. The literary day classes are under Dr. Ryland; a class in grammar, in arithmetic, in geography, and all in spelling and reading. With these classes he occupies himself from nine to three o'clock, alternately.

"I have a class of pastors and preachers with whom I spend an hour and a half daily. I have gone mostly through the Book of Hebrews. We first read a chapter, and I take great pains to have them read properly, slowly, naturally, distinctly, minding the pauses, observing proper emphasis, intonation, pronunciation, etc. Then I seize upon the points of

Gospel truth consecutively, in the order of Apostolic argument, and try to make them understand it as well as I can. Progress is very slow, and much patience is required. They have never been taught to think consecutively. We take any good young man, whether looking to the ministry or not. Most learn well. Some do not. I exercise a sovereign prerogative to dismiss the hopeless. But I said in the beginning no rule can be given you. You must 'cut and try.' My suggestions will be useless. Your own observations must guide you. Our work is a hard, but an important one."

During my first year in Richmond I was in frequent correspondence with Dr. Colver. As his health failed, these letters became less frequent. The following, dated Chicago, March 19th, 1869, shows the depth of his Christian affection and his interest in all that pertains to the Kingdom of Christ:

"How I would love to be with you. I became very much attached to those dear people. I rejoice in the conversion of Brother Armistead. Uncle Jeff and Aunty I love very much. I found Brother and Sister Holmes, all I could wish. They were so kind. I wish you to express to them how much I love them. * * * * * I ever trusted my papers and money in the hands of Brother Holmes, and ever found him true and upright. Remember me to Brother Jackson and to Brother Wells. They, with all the students, did all they could to make me happy. I hope you will find the same kindness at their hands. This is a glorious work. I am glad I engaged in it, though I have no doubt it was such an over-draught upon my bodily powers as to bring me to an early grave. I have got to die, but it will not be death. I shall pass over dry shod. Death in the Master's service or in His work of preaching the Gospel to the poor is a privilege. I think my work is done, and that it only remains for me hereafter to suffer the will of God. But I want the work done and it needs to be done quickly. The time will soon come when that School must be put upon a permanent basis and properly endowed, when we shall want to work into the Board much of the colored element. Train them for it as fast as you can. I never expect to be well again. I think a few months will send me home. Commend me to Brother Holmes, to the First Church, and to individual friends when you have the opportunity. I love to hear from you. No one to whom you write will sympathize with you as I do. The Lord Jesus sustain and help you in your great work. * * * May God strengthen us all to do and suffer all his will."

On the 22d of January, 1869, the Executive Committee of the National Theological Institute, "in honor of its first teacher and a life long friend of the slave and the freedmen," adopted the following resolution: That the School at Richmond be here-hereafter be designated "Colver Institute."

After mature and prayerful deliberation, at the annual meeting of the denomination in 1867, and onward, it was finally decided by mutual agreement that the work of the National Theological Institute should be merged into that of the American Baptist Home Mission Society. Formal action was taken when the anniversaries were held in Boston, May 19th, 1869, and eventually the Board of Managers transferred the work of the National Theological Institute to the American Baptist Home Mission Society, which adopted the schools and teachers as its own.

On May 26th, 1870, the American Baptist Home Mission Society, at the annual meeting in Philadelphia, resolved to petition Congress to declare null and void the charter of the National Theological Institute and University, and appointed Rev. J. B. Simmons, J. D. Fulton and G. W. Samson to lay the subject in a proper manner before Congress.

Dr. Peck,* the Corresponding Secretary, in his final official letter, dated May 22d, says: "My official connection ceased on Thursday. The changes which have been made and which are to be, I heartily concur in, and trust that they will eventuate in those great ends for which we are laboring."

---

* Rev. Solomon Peck, D. D., for many years was Corresponding Secretary of the American Baptist Missionary Union. He succeeded Dr. Parker as Secretary of the National Theological Institute and University.

Of this transfer of the work of the National Institute, official notice was sent by Dr. J. S. Backus, Corresponding Secretary of the American Baptist Home Mission Society, May 28, 1869, to Rev. C. H. Corey and Miss Hannah W. Goodman, as follows: "As the work of the National Theological Institute has now passed into the hands of the American Baptist Home Mission Society, you are requested, if agreeable to you, to make out your reports for the month of May to the Secretaries of the Home Mission Society, No. 39 Park Row, New York, and they will forward your month's salary."

The following from Dr. Peck's final report gives an account of our first year's work in the Colver Institute:

"Reports of the condition and progress of the School during the entire academic year have been regular, frequent and abundantly satisfactory. A just estimate of its general character and of its claims to support, may be derived from the quarterly report, submitted at the close of the second term. Mr. Corey then wrote, March 31st, 'Since our session commenced in October, one hundred and ninety-five have been in attendance at our School for a longer or shorter period. This number includes a night class of forty-five adults. During the term Miss Goodman, the popular and efficient associate teacher, has given instruction in reading, writing, arithmetic, spelling, geography and English grammar. There have been exercises in declamation and composition. The theological class has examined the Evidences of Christianity, has studied carefully portions of the Old and New Testaments, and has had weekly exercises in the composition and delivery of sermons. Lectures have been delivered to them on Interpretation and Biblical Antiquities. In addition to this they have had the benefit of Dr. Parker's admirable lectures. Two Latin classes and one Greek class have recited daily for three months past. Cæsar and Sallust have been read a portion of the time. Xenophon will be commenced shortly.

'It has been the aim of the instructors simply not to insist on studious habits in the students, but they have striven to develop every manly quality; they have aimed to make men of their pupils; God-fearing, self-denying men.

'The conduct of the students, generally, has been all that could be desired. Never could men work harder, or apply themselves more closely. Scarcely one has been absent or late at morning prayers or a recitation since the commencement of the term. We cannot thank too cordially the many friends who have so kindly remembered us with supplies of bedding and clothing. Many prayers ascend daily from this place on behalf of the friends of the School. May God bless them all.'"

The exhibit thus given is fully sustained by representations of brethren who have visited it, both of the North and the South, several of whom have left substantial tokens of the interest thus created or quickened. To use the words of Dr. Parker, "Brother Corey and his assistant are taking hold of the people. They have matters in excellent order. If the patrons of the Institute could look in upon the school each one would enlist recruits and gain contributions to the cause. To some of the ministers it seems an almost intolerable privation to lose a lesson."

## CHAPTER VII.

*Letter of Dr. Simmons on Lumpkin's Jail—Recollections by Mrs. H. Goodman-Smith—Purchase of the United States Hotel—Incorporated as Richmond Institute.*

BEFORE taking final leave of the Old Jail, we will introduce here letters from Dr. Simmons,* of New York, and Mrs. H. Goodman-Smith.

LUMPKIN'S SLAVE JAIL, BY JAMES B. SIMMONS, D. D.

Did Northern Baptists design to humiliate Southern Baptists, by using Lumpkin's Slave Jail, at the opening of their Freedmen School-work in Richmond, Virginia? No, the farthest from it. I remember that it was so hinted at the time. Some may still believe it. But I am glad to be able to

---

*James B. Simmons, D. D., one of the Secretaries of the American Baptist Home Mission Society, had charge of the Southern Department of its work, and of its educational work. This and similar institutes in the South, which he so successfully assisted in building up, are monuments to his marvellous and unremitting energy; and the solicitude with which he watched over them and the fidelity with which he studied their best interests, bear testimony to his absorbing interest in the welfare of the freedman, and the progress of the Kingdom of Christ.

show that the occupancy of those premises was wholly providential.

I will begin by saying that Baptists were not responsible for the existence of slavery. They did not originate it. Nor can they be held accountable for its bad features. True Baptists are true Christians, and true Christians all through the South are supposed to have done all that they could in the circumstances, even while slavery still existed, to ameliorate the hard features of that hard bondage. Nobody can deny that the institution of slavery was a very cruel one. So much so, that one eminent writer describes it as the "*sum of all villainies.*" It was certainly of the evil one, and not at all of Christ; for it was compelled to employ cruel agencies in order to maintain its power, not to say its existence. Hence the slave-hunter and the slave-ship for capturing its victims. Hence the slave-driver and the slave-whip. Hence the bloodhound, for runaways, and the slave-pen and the slave-jail, and the whipping ring for the incorrigible and the refractory.

True Christians in the South, as well as in the North, deplored these things and prayed against them. And it was in answer to these prayers, both in the North and in the South and in the other parts of the world, that slavery in these United States was brought to an end, in that year of wondrous grace to our brethren in bonds—1865. God did it by means of war; war so long and so bloody "that each drop drawn by the lash was repaid by another drop drawn by the sword;" but the *emancipating feature* of the war was in *answer to prayer beyond all doubt*. The reader will notice that I speak of the prayers of *true* Christians. Unconverted, irreligious church members, who still love the world and its wicked spirit and its cruel ways, are not Christians at all. They are sinners. Sometimes the worst of sinners. And God heareth not sinners. These sinners prayed for the continuance of slavery, and God refused their prayers. True Christians, on the other hand, are those who have been born again, " born from above," " born of the spirit," and who love God and their slave-neighbor as they love themselves, having the spirit of Christ. There were undoubtedly thousands of these Christians (whites as well as blacks) scattered over the slave States before the war. I knew personally a few such. I could *name* some of them; in the Carolinas, in Mississippi, in Kentucky, they dwelt, all of them whites. One of them from South Carolina, who emancipated his slaves long before the war, was afterwards a guest in my house for many days here in the North. And lovingly did we converse. There were also many other white slaveholders substantially of his spirit; tender hearted, but timid, who loved their slaves and pitied them and treated them beautifully, and would have freed them joyfully had they only known how. These all prayed secretly but fervently before the war for the overthrow of slavery, and after two hundred and fifty years God startled the whole world by the suddenness and bountifulness and magnificence of His answer. And so, when the war ended the slave was free. "The regime of the lash had gone; the regime of the spelling book had come." But how to *apply* the spelling book was the question. By the laws of the slave States it had long been a crime to teach a black man letters. By the laws of Jesus Christ all men, black and white alike, were to "search the scriptures." But how many white Christians were there in the South immediately after the war, when bad passions were still rampant, when hate prevailed and not love, who would have dared to sell a building or even lease a building in the face of their pro-slavery neighbors to be used as a school for negroes? In some localities, indeed, the negroes themselves were too timid to allow their own church-houses to be so used. The experience of Dr. Nathaniel Colver and of others proves this. And I myself, as late as 1870, five years after the war had closed, saw white property owners in Southern cities almost turn pale with fear when I asked them to sell me a piece of land for one of the Home Mission Society's colored schools. They would exclaim: "No, no. Never, never. My neighbors would blame me." One man said to me: "Sir, the price of that land is one thousand dollars an acre, but as you want it for a Negro School, you cannot have it at *any* price!"

Again, in many of the slave States before the civil war, and I presume it was so in Virginia, even *free* blacks, of which there were always a few, could not hold property except by means of *white trustees*. And church property owned by slaves, as for example, the First African Baptist Church, of Richmond, Virginia, must have been held for said slaves in the same way. So strict was the law in regard to the assembling of blacks, that no congregation or even considerable number of them could meet, even for the purposes of worshipping God, unless a white man was present in said assembly.

In the light of the above facts listen now to the story of Lumpkin's Jail and its occupancy by the American Baptist Home Mission Society for school purposes. Dr. Nathaniel Colver, above referred to, was a famous anti-slavery champion. For many years he was pastor at Tremont Temple in Boston, where he thundered with true Christian eloquence against all the sins in the Decalogue; especially against the saloon system and the system of human slavery. At the same time he preached Jesus most tenderly and effectively to the saving of great numbers of souls. Dr. Colver told me that when the war was over and the slave was free, that he felt like one who had been rescuing a drowning man in mid-winter. He had gotten his man out of the water onto the ice, as he expressed it, but the poor fellow would freeze to death if not looked after. So, said he, I started for Richmond to look after my freed-man. My plan was to open a school in one of the colored churches and instruct these preachers in the word of God. But the freedmen were timid. They were afraid of schools. They had never had any schools. Slavery had taught them that schools and book learning were not for the black man, but only for the whites. Both the colored pastors and the colored deacons stood in doubt therefore as to the wisdom of my plans. So, in my perplexity and straits, I devoted a day to fasting and prayer. And as the evening of that day approached, I went out of my place of prayer on to the streets of Richmond to see what answer the Lord might give me. I had not walked far when I met upon the sidewalk a group of colored people. I stopped them. I engaged them in conversation. I told them the story of my errand in Richmond and the obstacles I had encountered. In the midst of that group was a large, fair-faced freed-woman, nearly white, who said that *she* had a place which she thought I could have. The place proved to be the famous Lumpkin's Slave Jail, and this woman who owned it was the widow of Lumpkin, the slave dealer. Yes, the lawful widow. For though Lumpkin was a white man and had bought this woman many years before as a slave, and she had become the mother of his children, yet, after Richmond fell, he did the honorable thing of marrying her, and so legitimatized her and her children.

Thus they became his lawful heirs. Mrs. Lumpkin was a pious and intelligent woman, and after her marriage was admitted to membership in the First African Baptist Church of Richmond. For years before the war, so I was told, this slave-mother of the white jailer's children united with Lumpkin in sending their children to the North to school, winter after winter. The last I heard of them they were residing in one of the Northern States. Whether they pass as colored or whites I do not know. But I presume no trace could be found of them under the name of Lumpkin; for in the very nature of things they would be more than willing that all records and recollections of their birthplace and pedigree should be blotted out forever.

The narrative as given above I had partly from the lips of Dr. Colver himself, and partly from Baptists in Richmond who were personally acquainted with the Lumpkin household.

Lumpkin's slave-pen consisted of about half an acre of land near the center of the older portion of Richmond. The patch lay very low in a deep hollow or "bottom," as it might be called, through which a small stream of water ran very slowly. In reaching this place of sighs from Broad Street, one had to climb down the incline of a sandy embankment nearly one hundred feet. The descent was steep, irregular, and in places difficult. In approaching the place from the Franklin Street side, the descent was quite gradual and easy by means of a narrow, crooked, untidy lane. Around the outer borders of the said half acre was a fence, in some places ten or twelve feet in height. Inside of the fence, and very close to it, was a tall old brick building which Lumpkin had used for his dwelling-house. Near by were other buildings, also of brick, where he used to shelter the more peaceable of his slave-gangs that were brought to him from time to time to be sold. But in the center of the plot was the chief object of interest—a low, rough, brick building known as the "slave jail." In this building Lumpkin was accustomed to imprison the disobedient and punish the refractory. The stout iron bars were still to be seen across one or more of the windows during my repeated visits to this place. In the rough floor, and at about the center of it, was the stout iron staple and whipping ring.

It was in this old jail—this place of horrible memories to the blacks—that I found that noble man of God, Rev. Charles H. Corey, engaged in teaching a company of freedmen preachers. Dr. Colver, far advanced in years, had now withdrawn, and Brother Corey was his successor. In the tall old dwelling-house of the late Mr. Lumpkin, Dr. Corey kept house with his devoted, self-sacrificing, New England wife. I was their guest. They were happy in the work and so was I. For hideous as were the surroundings, a whole race had been born in a day into liberty. In the other buildings above alluded to, colored students for the ministry were living and boarding in common. They too were happy. Glad faces greeted me on every side. The old slave pen was no longer the "devil's half acre" but God's half acre. As Corresponding Secretary of the American Baptist Home Mission Society, I had repeatedly come to Richmond to purchase better quarters for this Christian School. And when it was announced to the fifty students that I had succeeded in buying the United States Hotel, on Main Street, their enthusiasm scarcely knew any bounds. Never shall I forget their beaming black faces and their eyes glistening with joy when Dr. Corey and I told them the following:

*First*—That the great hotel originally cost $110,000.

*Second*—That such was the changed state of things that the owners were glad enough to throw off the fraction of $100,000 and sell it to the Society for $10,000.

*Third*—That it would however require several thousand dollars over and above the purchase money to fit it up and furnish it for school purposes, and consequently—

*Fourth*—We *must* have the colored people help financially.

Then the prompt and generous way in which they pledged themselves to help was wonderful. Several said they would earn and give five dollars apiece. Others pledged ten dollars. Still others twenty, twenty-five, and fifty dollars each. Every student was requested to say a few words if he chose in reference to the purchase of the new property, and the hopes he had for himself and his people in connection with this school. All spoke in loud praise of Dr. Colver and Dr. Corey and of their assistant teachers. Rev. James H. Holmes, then as now the pastor of the First Colored Baptist Church in Richmond, a church of 4,000 members, was one of the pupils in this Lumpkin's Jail School, and spoke for himself and his people admirably. So did Richard Wells, pastor of the Ebenezer Baptist Church, and others too numerous to mention. One man, whose name I have forgotten, made quite a lengthy speech, and as he sat down pledged himself to help "right smart." I knew well enough that "right smart" was a Southern provincialism, and that it meant a "good deal." But as Dr. Corey had given the assembled school into my hands, so that I was presiding on this historic occasion, I insisted on knowing how much "right smart" meant in dollars and cents. After hesitating somewhat and blushing as well as an African young man well could, he replied that it meant "about fifty dollars." This elicited applause, of course, and I told the students that, though I did not like the phrase because it seemed to savor of slang, nevertheless they might use it freely at the rate of fifty dollars a time, till our newly-purchased school quarters should be put in good repair, furnished, and occupied free of debt.

I remember that Isaac P. Brockenton, a colored young pastor, from Darlington, South Carolina, also a pupil, was present on this memorable occasion. He told us that he had already built a meeting-house for his people since the war closed, the first offering towards it being twenty-five cents which he himself contributed. He gave us a most vivid picture of how he led his people to victory from so small a beginning as that. How his church members at first laughed to scorn his poor little twenty-five cent piece as it lay there lonesome upon the table; and how a year later they cried for joy, and sang and shouted triumphantly over their little meeting-house, built and paid for by a great many twenty-five cent gifts, which they themselves had brought in. It is not at all to be wondered at that this same man Brockenton, child of God and brother of Jesus and hero of faith, as a grain of mustard seed, has since built two other Baptist Churches in his own town of Darlington, the last one costing $18,000.

It is such men as these, Holmes, Wells, Brockenton, and many others, that Dr. Corey and his able Faculty have been training for the past twenty-five years. And I am proud of them. They are my brothers in Christ, and I have not so much as a *shred* of sympathy for the man who despises them.

To slur them, to harm them, is to slur and harm Jesus.

So nobly did the colored students and the colored churches and people of Richmond and Virginia come up to the help of the Lord in this crisis, that it awakened great enthusiasm all through the North, and among the white Christians in the South as well. And here let me say that just in proportion as the freedmen brethren deny themselves in all unwise and wasteful personal and family expenditures, and give largely and liberally to the Home Mission Society for the building up of these young colleges, just in that proportion will they receive more and more help from their brethren of the white race all over the land. *Men love to help those that help themselves.* Let the negroes therefore make Wesley's motto their motto, viz: "To EARN all they can, SAVE all they can, and GIVE all they can."

It was a proud day when the students and teachers of Lumpkin's Jail marched up out of that old slave-pen, and took possession of the United States Hotel, at the corner of Nineteenth and Main Streets. That noble property, once the fashionable hotel of Richmond, so ample and so admirable in all its appointments, had now been thoroughly cleaned and repaired, and furnished with new school furniture, and was joyfully dedicated to its new and sacred uses with hymns of praise and songs of thanksgiving to God. It is still in use under the name of the Richmond Theological Seminary, and Dr. Corey is the honored President.

He who began as the despised teacher of negroes (despised only by the worst people, never by the best) has been heard from since. Twenty-seven years ago he was an unknown young man commencing a work for Jesus Christ, in the spirit of Jesus Christ, and nothing could daunt him. Sheltered beneath the roof of an abandoned slave jail, the best quarters he and his poor freedmen-students could for the time being command, he cheerfully bided his time. He seems never to have pined for social recognition; he was too busy. If the roughs jeered him on the streets, he not only bore it patiently, but answered them back with a benevolent smile. And this habit of tossing back loving smiles to those unfriendly to his work on the New Testament plan, has left dimples in Dr. Corey's cheeks. If anybody doubts it, let him engage the genial Doctor in conversation about the amusing occurrences of those early days of his life in Richmond, and those same benevolent dimples will reappear upon his face.

Since those early days he has received four times in succession the complimentary title of Doctor of Divinity from four different colleges. Two of these colleges are Northern and two are Southern. And the two in the South, I am glad to say, viz: Richmond College, in Virginia, the very spot where he has done his life work of love, and Baylor University, in Texas, were several years in advance of the two Northern Colleges in bestowing these well merited honors upon this devoted son of Christ.\*

RECOLLECTIONS BY MRS. H. G. SMITH, A FORMER TEACHER IN COLVER INSTITUTE.

Mrs. H. Goodman-Smith † provides some interesting reminiscences of her four years connection with the School in Richmond:

"The first two years in Richmond we were located at Lumpkin's Jail, where our sessions were

---

\*The writer protested two or three times against the last paragraphs in the letter of Dr. Simmons, deeming them unnecessary. But Dr. Simmons insists on his "rights as the author of the article to have it appear in its integrity," as he wrote it. He adds, under date of September 27th, 1894, just after the death of his accomplished and devoted wife:

"I am eager to see your book. When will it come? How I wish my precious wife could have seen it. She took the most profound interest in you and your wife and your noble work. Neither you of the Richmond School, nor the teachers of any of the seven schools I helped to establish, will ever know your indebtedness to that loving, praying, faithful wife, who at length rests from her labors and her works do follow her."

† Miss Goodman was a lady of culture and refinement. After four years of efficient and self-denying service at Richmond, and three years at Benedict Institute, Columbia, South Carolina, she was transferred to Leland University, New Orleans, Louisiana, where she remained one year. She was subsequently married to Mr. W. H. Smith. Their comfortable home at Rockford, Illinois, was always open to weary missionary workers. Mr. Smith was a helper of all worthy causes, and was especially interested in the work for the colored people.

held, while the teachers occupied rooms in another building on the premises. So entirely absorbed were we in our arduous work of teaching these eager students, some of whom were already pastors, that our uninviting surroundings were unthought of by us, only as our Northern friends commented on them in their visits to us. In addition to teaching, there was the distribution of clothing and bedding to the needy, and general missionary work, with the giving of concerts for the benefit of the students.

"An afternoon class, consisting in all of eighty, many of whom were mothers and some grandmothers, was conducted by Mrs. Corey and myself. These earnest women highly appreciated their opportunity, and rejoiced greatly when they had learned to read ' the Word.'

" In a recent visit to the Richmond Theological Seminary, I could but contrast the students of to-day with those of twenty-six years ago. I was amazed at the development of character, the sound thought, the readiness of expression, and the refinement in manners, and the neatness of person of those I saw. These results must have come from hard and persistent personal labor.

"Among the visitors to our Institute was Hon. Henry Bill, of Norwich, Connecticut. Though a Congregationalist, he became deeply interested in our work. He remarked that ' he would rather see his son the President of such an Institution for colored people than to see him the President of the United States.'

"Mr. Bill gave largely of the books he published, both to the Library of the School and also to some of the Sunday-schools in Richmond. One of our pupils, J. E. Jones, had become nearly prepared for college. Mr. Bill furnished the money for his expenses for nearly five years at Madison University, the rest being secured by me from my personal friends. After graduating with honor, Prof. Jones has been for nineteen years a teacher in the Institution of which he was formerly a pupil. Prof. Vassar also was graduated from Madison University, and for eighteen years has been a teacher in the Institution where he entered as a pupil, then being unable to write his name.

"I shall never forget 'Uncle Jeffry' and his faithful services, and his devotion to the services of the Master. I am reminded by my friend, Mrs. Sarah Hanson Nichols, a generous friend of the Seminary, and my present hostess as I write, of an incident which occurred during a visit she paid at Richmond. Uncle Jeffry, while attending to some service in my room, seeming unconscious of our presence, said half aloud, 'Last night I had a vision; and the old woman (meaning his recently departed wife) was there, I seed her plain as I'se looking at you wid dese two eyes; she was a walking the golden streets wid her silver slippers on. Dar wasn't a black one thar. Dey had all been

washed in de blood of de Lam; and made clean and white as snow. And she said, "yonder, dar he's coming, Old Jeffry." Another time he met me coming out of the Schoolroom, and said, 'Its heaps of burdens you're a toting on your shoulders for my poor down-trodden race, and I prays for you and Dr. Corey every day. If anybody in de world ought to get de blessing it is you, sure nuff.' One evening while coming from his praying meeting he said to me, 'How did you like my meeting?' I replied, 'Very much, did'nt you?' 'No,' he said, 'dar was so many prayers and *not a single grunt*, mighty cold Missus, mighty cold, so many prayers and *not a single grunt*.' He was accustomed to sing with great pathos and power his favorite hymns, 'we'll walk tru de valley in peace if Jesus His self be our leader dar,' and 'Hark from de tooms a doleful sound.'

"Uncle Jeff had been a hard worker. He was bent and crippled and almost toothless. He had been owned by a man who was very cruel, and who, under the disappointment of losing his three hundred slaves, hanged himself at the close of the war. Dr. Parker said to him: 'And how did you feel, Uncle Jeff, when your old master was dead?' With his hand on his mouth, he said, 'You see, Doctor, I tried to be resigned,' but the merry twinkle in his eye and the suppressed *te, he, he*, showed that, to say the least, his grief had not lasted very long.

"In reviewing the past I recall my visit to Dr. Colver, at Chicago, a short time before he died. He asked me about James H. Holmes, the good, strong man, who gave promise of being a power in the church, and Richard Wells, so reliable and trustworthy. His farewell messages were sent to his beloved pupils, and his congratulations to Dr. Corey for his successes.

"Be assured that though my connection with the Institution has long since ceased, my thoughts will always center there, and my best wishes will follow the President and students, and I believe, as did my departed husband, that it is the best conducted school of its kind that we ever visited."

As the lease of Lumpkin's Jail was to expire in 1870, it became necessary to secure a more permanent location. The United States Hotel (until 1853 known as the Union Hotel) on the corner of 19th and Main Streets, was purchased January 26th, 1870, and in the fall of the same year the building was occupied by the school. The main building, which is of brick, fronts sixty-two feet on Main Street and fifty feet on Nineteenth Street. It is four stories high. An L, one hundred feet long and thirty-nine feet wide, runs along Nineteenth Street. The building was erected in 1818, and it was at the time the most fashionable hotel of Richmond. It contains about fifty rooms. The property is said to have cost originally $110,000. It was purchased for $10,000.

In this part of the city in those days were the homes of the prosperous and fashionable families. The hotel was the stopping place of the most distinguished people of the State. The members of the General Assembly who boarded there did not dine with the ordinary guests, but took their meals entirely by themselves. After the building ceased to be a hotel, it was used as a medical college. In the days of the war it was a Confederate Hospital. Immediately after the war a school for colored children was taught in its largest rooms.

The Freedmen's Bureau, from the funds appropriated to "erection, rental and repair of school houses," furnished the money. Rev. R. M. Manly was at this time State Superintendent of Education under the Freedmen's Bureau, and actively promoted the interests of the school. The trustees were A. B. Capwell, James B. Simmons, J. S. Backus, E. E. L. Taylor, Albert Brooks, Henry K. Ellyson and R. M. Manly.

After obtaining possession of the building it was solemnly dedicated to God. In one of the uppermost rooms we knelt with Secretary Simmons, and besought God's blessing upon the building and upon the work of Christian Education, for which it was to be used. Extensive repairs were needed; many of the windows were boarded up; the pigeons had taken possession of some of the rooms, and the plastering had fallen in many others of them.

After the duties of the school were over, the students in the old jail hastened daily with alacrity to the newly-purchased building, and in various ways assisted in repairing it; they contributed fully a thousand dollars' worth of labor. They also gave of their own means. They went through the city, and from people, both white and colored, they collected a $1,000. This was secured in small sums, and the list containing the names of contributors was more than six yards in length.

The School for a long time had been familiarly known as "THE COLVER INSTITUTE," but for satisfactory reasons the more general name, "THE RICHMOND INSTITUTE," was inserted in the deed which conveyed the property to the Trustees, and under that name it was incorporated by an act passed by the General Assembly of Virginia, February 10th, 1876.

On November 22d, 1876, the Trustees met in New York City, and organized under the provisions of the very liberal charter which had been granted them, exempting from taxation property to the amount of $500,000.

RICHMOND THEOLOGICAL SEMINARY.

## CHAPTER VIII.

*Extracts from Official Letters of Secretaries—Extracts from other Letters—Needy Students.*

THE following extracts from letters from Secretary Simmons of the American Baptist Home Mission Society, and from others, will give some idea of the growth and development of the work:

"NOVEMBER 3D, 1869.

"I want you to ask God, the great and rich God, for the sake of his son Jesus, to help you find one or several of his stewards, who will give $25,000 to endow the Colver Institute. Work among those who love, and will be glad to honor, the name of that prince among men, Nathaniel Colver.

"J. B. SIMMONS."

"FEBRUARY 12TH, 1870.

"But God will give us the money, and it will pay large returns. Let us have faith, and so please Jesus. We shall soon stand in His presence with our work done. J. B. S."

"FEBRUARY 12TH, 1870.

"To get money you must open your mouth wide, like a young robin swallowing a big grasshopper whole. \* \* \* \* You do not know how the burdens have accumulated upon me since I have left you. My heart is absorbed with a desire, irrepressible and painful, to found a school like yours, and in a building as good as yours, in every one of these Southern States. To this grand work I must give myself. Hence, I shall have to leave you and your students the work of putting that building in order. Tell the students so. Lay the heavy burden on them. Have no scruples. Tell them I want to know what they will amount to when they become pastors, when each one ought to raise from $5,000 to $25,000 alone in building meeting houses, if all of them together cannot now raise this small sum of $5,000. J. B. S."

In the following extract reference is made to subscriptions secured by the students for the necessary repairs of the building on the corner of Nineteenth and Main Streets. The list was more than six yards long:

"April 5th, 1870.

"You do not know how pleased I am with the three yards and one-half of names you send me. I have measured, and three and a half is the number. Add to the list when you get another yard of them. A yard at a time is what I desire you to send. * * You are doing nobly. Keep on. Tell the students I am greatly pleased with what they have done. Let none be discouraged. Everyone will reap at length if he faint not. Everyone. Tell them I say so. But my saying is of little account. God's word says so. J. B. S."

"June 13th, 1870.

"Ever dear Brother, I wish you to know that we rejoice exceedingly at the success the Lord has given you in Richmond. As the colored people voted by a unanimous uprising to pray for you and help you, so do we. * * * * These colleges for colored preachers, like the whites, cannot be carried along with real power unless they can have the benefit of permanent endowment funds. We expect you to prove yourself, by God's help, the author and organizer of a great success in Richmond. J. B. S."

"July 7th, 1870.

"As an encouragement to you, let me say that, after applying day after day, by laborious effort, to some forty persons, being turned off shortly and again even rudely, God brought me at length to one of His hidden saints, who said, before I had finished stating the great work, 'My brother, I think the Lord sent you here. I have money and I want to give it. I want to be mainly my own executor.' That person has already paid into our treasury several thousand dollars, and more are coming.

"J. B. S."

"September 16th, 1870.

"Be careful to spend no money on bad material

in students. Even a house of worthless bricks tumbles down. A chief donor just now says, 'I give cheerfully to them. But they must dig as I had to.' Another, who recently gave several thousands to our Freedmen Fund, worked his way through college, and is indignant at any thought of shiftlessness on the part of those students whom he is helping. He is terribly in earnest. J. B. S."

"DECEMBER 27TH, 1870.

"All day long I have been treading these streets to collect funds for your school, and no man has given me a dollar. Tell your students this. Tell them that my faith is such, however, that if forty-nine refuse me, that I believe the fiftieth man will give me at least one dollar. Has God given them such faith as this, and are they thus at work? Some are, I know. Everyone of them should be. Tell them I say so. Tell them to pray for me as I pray for them. We are all in partnership, and Jesus is the Head of the Firm. J. B. S."

"JANUARY 7TH, 1871.

" While He blesses me, and your teachers work and bear burdens, you must bear burdens too. Those at the North who give, charge me to tell you so. You must help. Everyone of you. I want, 1st. That you should pray a great deal more. By *ones* as directed in Matt. vi, 6 and by *twos* as in Matt. xviii, 19. Pray about this particular matter of *more money*.  2d. I want everyone of you who can to pay partly or wholly for your own board from this day onward.  3d. I want you to help to save expenses of fuel and lights and everything.  4th. I want you to go kindly and with cheerful courage to the poor and the rich and liberal Christians of Richmond, of all denominations, and ask for aid. Go also to the men of the world.    J. B. S."

"February 3d, 1871.

"I have great pleasure in your School.  I pray for you much.  And upon every remembrance of yourself and wife, and your teachers and your pupils, I say: 'God bless them every one.'  * * * We pray for the donors to your School often.

"J. B. S."

"February 24th, 1871.

"Do not think for a moment of leaving Richmond.  There is no field on earth where you can be more useful, in my judgment, or see greater results of your labor.  But be careful; do not overwork.  Take whatever rest is needed each day. Don't wait until vacation.  That is often fatal. But don't give up the work at Richmond on any account.  You have your hand in, God has blessed you in the work, and I am confident that He will still bless you in it.  It is the blessing of the Lord that maketh rich, and He addeth no *sorrow* therewith.    J. B. S."

"SEPTEMBER 15TH, 1871.

"It was on the 12th inst. *Resolved*, 'That the Board finds it indispensable that the teachers of freedmen schools keep a constant and watchful eye to the raising of funds; and that the principals and male assistants, specially, be requested to give their energies each Sabbath to preaching or delivering addresses, and taking subscriptions and collections for the freedmen's educational work of this Society.' As you have done this all along, you will, I know, cheerfully keep on as your own strength may warrant.   *   *   *   If all worked as heartily and earnestly as you in collecting, our Board would not need to pass many resolutions.        J. B. S."

"OCTOBER 31ST, 1871.

"Lending does not seem to me to be much encouraged in the Bible. I know it says, 'Do good and lend,' but it is added, 'hoping for nothing again,' which makes it much the same as giving. It is the way the ignorant poor impoverish themselves, this *miserable*, MISERABLE, MISERABLE habit they have of lending to irresponsible and dishonest people without taking legal written security. One of our colored students has from $100 to $300 thus loaned, and behold we have to feed him or turn him out of school.        J. B. S."

"JANUARY 8TH, 1872.

"Let us keep up good heart. At times, with

the pressure of this work upon me, my heart grows sad. But it ought not to be so. I am ashamed that it is so, for God has the supervision of this work. The more than one hundred laborers in the South half of our field, whose salaries are more or less dependent upon my efforts, are every one very dear to God. He loves them. He is in the field with them. He defends them. And though I am irreligiously anxious at times, I am glad to tell you that it is sweet to me to commend them daily to God's care; and of the whole one hundred none more so than yourself and your wife and your fellow-teachers. J. B. S."

The following letter has reference to seventeen students who were appointed as missionaries in Virginia during the summer of 1872. Fifteen had also been appointed and served during the summer of 1871:

"May 16th, 1872.

"Your telegram is received. Enclosed find our check for eighty-five dollars, in advance on salaries of your seventeen student-missionaries, to help them to their fields. Report to J. M. Whitehead at once, please, just how much you paid to each. Some may need more than others. Enclosed in another envelope we send you the seventeen commissions and a copy of 'Principles and Purposes' for each one. J. B. S."

"OCTOBER 12TH, 1872.

"Your students made from forty-eight to three hundred visits each. Urge upon their attention Acts v, 42, and Acts xx, 20 in the matter of this household preaching. It is a vast power.

"J. B. S."

"NOVEMBER 30TH, 1872.

"No students thus far, as a whole, have equalled yours in raising funds. That is, your school of students have done more than any other school of students. Some individuals in the other schools have done as much or more, perhaps, than any one of yours. But God has greatly blessed and helped you in training your men to raise money. Do not lose your art. Do not let your school lose its prestige. Keep it ahead. 'Ole Virginny never tire.' * * * Go everywhere among your people and stir them up on this subject. Beg their money. Beg their prayers. Beg their sympathies. Preach on the subject; lecture on it and pray about it. The $1,000 you have raised will soon be increased to $2,000 if you heartily work together. J. B. S."

Our school at Richmond was the first among all the institutions of the South to employ colored teachers. They have now been in our institution for more than twenty years.

"DECEMBER 27TH, 1872.

"I was in hopes (and I do hope still) that your

colored assistants would prove a grand success. Your movement in that line is popular both with whites and blacks. You do not know how resolutely colored leaders have pressed us to employ and pay colored teachers. I do hope you will fight it out on this line. 'Look not back, nor tarry in all this plain.' I pray you take your strongest and ablest students (those who combine strong minds with broad, generous, loving hearts), and drill them, and *drill* them, and DRILL them privately, until they ache down to the very core of their hearts and marrow with a sense of their responsibility to God and their race. As to secular work, Paul made tents, and Jesus, the Son of God, himself wrought as a carpenter. Ministers who don't, lack one grand element of power. The example you set and the training you give to your students in secular matters is an all-important part of their education.

"J. B. S."

In response to an announcement to Dr. Simmons of a handsome donation by a Virginian, he writes:

"JANUARY 29TH, 1873.

"I doubt not there are full one hundred more in Virginia like him, or the equivalent of one hundred. Some can give more and some less. Tell your students this. Make it plain to them. And rouse them and charge them in the name of the Lord to find these one hundred. They can. You know how in your bold, kind, persuasive way, to teach them to do it. Out of about each forty persons applied to by me, one gives something. Tell them this. Can they expect it will fare better with them?

"J. B. S."

In a season of great financial depression, he writes:

"March 19th, 1873.

"In the circumstances, I would suggest three things: 1st. That you withdraw pecuniary help from students of doubtful worth, if you have any such on your list, whether you are helping them little or much. 2d. That school expenses be cut down as much as possible in other ways. 3d. That you lay these facts, as to the treasury, on the minds and hearts of your pupils and fellow-teachers, and that they all join us in praying God to help us to the needed means for carrying on all the schools during the coming year. J. B. S."

Referring to the appointment of Dr. Stone as special lecturer, he writes:

"April 16th, 1873.

"Rev. Mr. Stone, D. D., of Marietta, Ohio, was appointed at the last meeting of the Board to spend a few weeks in holding Ministerial Institutes for freedmen (students and others) and lecturing on practical and doctrinal theology, say in the schools from Washington to Augusta. I trust you will give the most *full, early* and *emphatic* announcements in all the churches and prayer-meetings; that you and your students will write cordial letters to men at a distance and get places of entertainment for them; that you and they will labor personally with all the pastors and leaders in and around Richmond to induce them to attend; and that you will secure eminent talent to render Dr. Stone such aid as he may need. J. B. S."

"OCTOBER 23D, 1873.

"I beg you, and your fellow-teachers and all your praying students, to make it a special point, day by day, to pray that God will give you the choicest spirits for pupils in your school. A school made up of such material, made up of such as God has called, set apart and annointed unto himself, is worth a thousand times more than a school made up of ordinary material. Please impress this on the minds of all who are about you who pray. I join you in these prayers. J. B. S."

The following from Secretary Taylor, who succeeded Dr. Simmons, shows what grave responsibilities rested upon the Principals of these Institutions while in their formative state:

"JULY 7TH, 1874.

"I must feel, as I do, that you know a hundred times more about our Richmond School than I and our Board united. I propose to *follow* you therefore, and if there are grave mistakes in the School at Richmond, Charles H. Corey must bear the responsibility, very largely, of them, and not I.

"E. E. L. TAYLOR, *Cor. Sec.*"

The following action was taken respecting Beneficiary Aid in the schools sustained by the Society:

"JANUARY 22D, 1879.

"*Resolved*, That the Board instruct the Principals that further beneficiaries should be received only on specific donations, or on authority previously received from the Board.

"S. S. CUTTING, *Cor. Sec.*"

The action respecting assisting students in the various institutions was reaffirmed. The following from Secretary Morehouse on this matter is official:

"MARCH 10TH, 1885.

"After June, 1885, no appropriations will be made for the support of beneficiaries in the schools beyond the amounts especially contributed and designated for that purpose." And again, July 17th, 1885, "We have decided to cut off any further appropriations from the funds of the Society for beneficiary aid. * * * * Unless the colored churches, or unless the friends of the colored people, will respond for the support of these men studying for the ministry, some of them will have to drop out of their course."

A conference was held in New York, June 4th, 1879, in which the interests of the Richmond Institute and the other schools were considered, in accordance with the following resolution:

"MARCH 10TH, 1879.

"*Resolved*, That the Principals of our Freedmen Schools be instructed to meet in convention with this Committee, to consider matters of vital importance relative to the successful prosecution of our educational work, the meeting to be held at these rooms on Wednesday, June 4th, 1879."

"S. S. CUTTING, *Cor. Sec*"

"JANUARY 31ST, 1880.

"In the fall of 1879 we received a communication from the Corresponding Secretary of the Virginia Baptist State Convention, Rev. E. G. Corprew, submitting to us the request of that body, viz: that we extend the Course of Instruction in Richmond Institute, and to so enlarge its facilities and accommodations as to admit female students. In December the Board referred the subject to the Corresponding Secretary of this Society, with the President of the Institute and its Board of Trustees.

"H. L. MOREHOUSE, D. D., *Cor. Sec.*"

In response to the request above referred to, with the approval of the Board in New York, the Richmond Institute admitted a limited number of young women. This was continued until the Hartshorn Memorial College for young women was opened in 1883.

The following letter refers to the purchase of a new site for buildings for the Institution:

"APRIL 14TH, 1880.

"The Board on Monday decided to purchase 'A' of Mr. Hoyt's property, as you will see by the enclosed letter to Mr. Hoyt, which, after reading, you will please deliver to him. The half of 'B' would, undoubtedly, be very desirable, and had we the means to invest in it, we might have favored its purchase. But 'A' will be a larger tract of land than either New York University or Columbia College own in this city. It is the decided conviction of Dr. Bishop and of the other members of the Educational Committee that one and three-quarters acres will be all that is necessary for school purposes. This is about the amount included in this tract. Buildings judiciously planned and located on these grounds, will afford ample accommodations for every school purpose. Certainly the location will be a vast change for the better over the present one, or over the original one by the slave mart. H. L. M., *Cor. Sec.*"

The following letters refer to the successful efforts made to secure the endowment of two Professorships in the Institution. In the spring of 1865, quite soon after the fall of Charleston, South Carolina, J. B. Hoyt and Rev. Dr. Lathrop visited that city. These gentlemen, who found me there in charge of the work of the United States Christian Commission, urged me to give myself to labor for the colored people of the State. I reminded Mr. Hoyt of this when I visited him with the view of securing this subscription. I told him that through his encouragement I had given my life to this work, and that he must stand by me and help me make the work a success. He contributed the sum of $25,000, and J. D. Rockefeller also contributed the sum of $25,000:

"JANUARY 29TH, 1884.

"I have good news for you. I have the promise of $25,000 for a Professorship of Theology in Richmond Institute, provided $25,000 for another Professorship can be raised by October 1st, 1884. So you see we have not been too fast in deciding to make this our first high grade theological school.

"H. L. M., *Cor. Sec.*"

"SEPTEMBER 15TH, 1884.

"Hallelujah! The second $25,000 is pledged by Mr. Hoyt. I wrote him a careful letter last week. He called at the rooms to-day and said that his wife and himself talked it over yesterday (Sunday) and decided to do it. Again hallelujah! Now for the third $25,000, according to our plan.

"H. L. M., *Cor. Sec.*"

### Extracts from Miscellaneous Letters.

Rev. Dr. White, now of the *Georgia Baptist*, visited our School, where he met Rev. James H. Holmes, who at that time was the pastor of the largest Baptist Church in the world, and yet was a pupil in the School, writes:

"Augusta, Ga., January 17th, 1870.

" I have never in my life had so deep an impression made upon me in the same length of time as during the twenty-four hours spent with you in Richmond; your school is ever before my eyes. The place, its former use, etc., are well calculated to illustrate the great change that has taken place in this country in the last few years. Bless the Lord, O my soul. Our Schools, under the Baptists, are doing splendidly. I have frequently spoken to our people of Brother Holmes. I think his example should be kept before our ministering brethren.   W. J. White."

The following shows the unabated interest of ex-Secretary Simmons in the work:

"January 26th, 1879.

" W. W. Colley is the first of Richmond Institute graduates who goes to Africa, and the first of the seven schools. Tell him to be to Africa what Judson was to Burmah. I am also glad to see that you have four others who are looking to Africa.

God bless them, every one, and make them hero missionaries. I was thrilled with delight the other day to learn that your students and other colored people have paid in full $2,000 at the Home Mission Rooms towards the endowment of Richmond Institute. Keep right on in that way, I entreat you; the endowment question is the vital question, next to the ordinary blessings of God.

"J. B. SIMMONS."

"NEW YORK, March 12th, 1877.

"Were I you, I would *emphasize*, EMPHASIZE, EMPHASIZE the matter of giving intelligence about *Africa* and praying for AFRICA and working for AFRICA. The school that does the most for that cause will be the most loved and the most helped by our people, and at the same time will not be a whit the less useful in raising up able and useful laborers for the home field. There is something about the cause of Home and Foreign Missions which enlarges the heart and broadens the sympathies and ennobles the whole being of man. How glad I am that you believe this and practice upon it. J. B. S."

The following letter from a brother beloved, who has toiled long and successfully, is introduced without apology:

"SEPTEMBER 27TH, 1880.

"I wish I could see you and talk with you about

our spiritual condition. I have fears that I have not faith enough for the work of the new year. Can there be positions where more real faith is needed? We must look far into the future and search out the plans of God. I feel weak and almost faithless. Won't you pray for me that I may overcome by faith? My influence over the men I want should be more potent. When I see these dull students filling honored positions, I wonder if I might not have been more to them if I had been filled more entirely with Christ. Do you ever feel that way? I have been reading 'Twenty-six Years in Burmah,' Dr. Binney's Life. Is God with me in my life as truly as He was with Dr. Binney? This is just as real mission work. Then, too, I think the School would gain more if I had the close union with God that I ought to have. The experience of the last four months has been a shadow over me. I failed in my plans. Was I selfish? Were my motives false? I want more power—the power that comes from a closer union with the Divine. My conflicts in taking up the work of the new year have been many."

The following letters are introduced to make known the struggles of men to fit themselves for usefulness. In the days of missionary service in South Carolina I organized the church over which Brother Govan at the same time was ordained pastor. In his old age he was seeking to "pick up a few crumbs" that he might be better able to teach his people:

"COLUMBIA, S. C., December 19th, 1871.

"At times I have not known at one meal where I could get the other. I have five in my family, one son sick, since dead, and only myself to work. My son died on the 27th of last June. I buried my daughter one year ago last February. The wife I had when you were with me is dead. They all died leaving good testimony of a hope of eternal life.

J. COREY GOVAN."

"COLUMBIA, S. C., February 15th, 1872.

"I am still at this Institute, but how long I shall stay I cannot say. I have now in my old age bought twenty-five acres of land, and I want to pay for it and get it cleared up. It is now all wood land, and I am the strongest one to do anything. I am now sixty-eight years old. By the grace of God I am holding on my way in the good work to which He has called me, getting weaker in body, but remain the same in spirit, loving the Lord and strong in the blessed Jesus. I am now here at the Benedict learning about God, and getting better able to read the Bible and preach the Gospel better and better. It is all from God, as is also this

GRADUATING CLASS, RICHMOND THEOLOGICAL SEMINARY.
1883.

School. I have labored hard to get the people to come, and have got some to come here and study. My dear brother, I look upon you as a father, as you have done more for me than any other white man.

"J. COREY GOVAN."

The following is from a freedman student for the ministry at Richmond. It was addressed to the friend who paid into the Home Mission Treasury fifty dollars for his board:

"DEAR FRIEND: I was a slave until the close of the war. I heard of this school last year, but did not have money to pay for my board.

"I have a wife and two children, but she thought that she could support the children while I was in school. So I started. I walked about 100 miles, and slept out of doors. I walked from noon one day until noon the next day without a bite of bread. But when I got here I was received kindly, though I had no money. I have on the clothes that my teacher gave me since I came. I never went to school a day before I came here, but I could read and write a little. I trust that I will never forget your kindness in time nor in eternity.

"Yours truly,

"HARVEY MORRIS."

From an applicant living in a distant State, for admission to Richmond Theological Seminary:

"I am engaged here in what I regard as missionary work. I am trying to make arrangements to enter school next session. I want to be thoroughly prepared for service among my people. But I have no means. I am out of money, out of clothes, out of doors. I am willing to do anything to help myself. If you can do nothing else for me, give me some advice."

## CHAPTER IX.

*Need of Enlightened Leaders—Extracts from Letters—
Difficulties—Early Encouragements—Drs. Dickinson
and Jeter—Other early Friends—An Amusing Incident—The Capitol Disaster.*

OF the importance of the work of educating the colored ministry, there can be but one opinion. I add here the expressions of distinguished men on this point.

The following eloquent passage is from the sermon of Rev. E. T. Winkler, D. D., an eminent Southern Baptist, of Charleston, S. C. It was delivered before the American Baptist Home Mission Society, at Chicago, in May, 1871. His theme was: "The Education of Colored Preachers." In closing his discourse, which gave great satisfaction, both to the men of the North and of the South, he said:

"And then Africa—Africa, of whom the millions of colored people in America are only the representatives; Africa, that land that holds the sorrows of vanished ages in its shadowy deeps; Africa, that mysterious unrecorded history of pestilences and famines and massacres, of degrading idolatries and sanguinary despotisms; Africa, that deadly region of fiery suns and oozy rivers that drive back the white man from its coasts of gold and pearl; Africa, that grave of missionaries lying yonder in ghastly despair beneath the pomp and glory of the tropics; Africa, that peopled world on which the light of prophecy falls and to which the grace of Christ extends; has she not loaned us her children for a little season that we may send them back to her, redeemed and regenerate, and that thus, through their means and ours, Ethiopia may stretch forth her dusky hands to God?

"Africa needs her children. She calls them back to her palmy coasts. As Rachel wept for Joseph, so she yearns for her exiled ones. As the man of Macedonia cried to Paul, she summons her apostles across the misty sea.

"Thus the education of a colored ministry inaugurates a vast missionary movement. With their advance in saving knowledge a countless host advances.

"The seminaries in which they are trained will nurse the churches of a continent; and their employment in the sphere to which they are called by the providence and the grace of Almighty God will tell upon the salvation of the world."

Dr. J. W. Parker, speaking in Tremont Temple, Boston, of the opportunity of usefulness, at the South, plead for the support of schools for ministers, and exclaimed with thrilling emphasis, "*I know*, I know *there never was, since Christ hung on the cross of Calvary, such an opportunity.* There has been no such day."

Rev. P. P. Bishop says: "The education of colored preachers is *the one great and crying need of the Freedmen!* Their preachers have unbounded influence over them."

Edward Lathrop, D. D., upon returning from a Southern tour, writes: "I would say emphatically, throw all you strength into schools for the education of a competent ministry. On this point I am afraid our churches are not *half* aroused. It is my deliberate and firm conviction that, if we fail in this, our work at the South, among the colored population, will come to a disastrous end. This, in so far as the freedmen are concerned, is the great work of the Home Mission Society. We *must* educate a ministry for this people, or abandon the field!"

J. M. Cramp, D. D., for many years the distinguished President of Acadia College, Nova Scotia, thus expresses his opinion as to the work in which his former pupil was engaged:

"Acadia College, Wolville, N. S.,
"January 23d, 1869.

"You are engaged in a good and very useful and important work, requiring great energy and much prudence—just such wisdom as the Lord has promised to give them that ask him. Past success encourages you. May the future be yet more blessed.

"J. M. Cramp."

The following letter is from Rev. T. Willard Lewis, a noble brother, who years ago entered into his rest, while engaged in missionary labor under the auspices of the Methodist Episcopal Church:

"Charleston, S. C., February 11th, 1871.

"I am glad to know that you have made such a success of Colver Institute, for the training of teachers and preachers. I believe you are doing ten times as much for Christ and His cause as you could possibly do as a pastor of a single church, and since we have but one short life to live, how grateful we should be in that God has opened this good and effectual door to us in this Southern field, though our labors and sacrifices are unappreciated, and sometimes received with ingratitude on the part of those for whom we toil and suffer reproach.

"T. W. Lewis."

Dr. S. F. Smith, the author of our "National Hymn," who, with his wife, spent two weeks at the Institution, writes:

"Newton Centre, Mass.,
"November 25th, 1877.

"And among the most cherished remembrances

of our month of travel, will ever be the enjoyment we experienced in being with you, in sympathizing in your difficulties and in rejoicing with you in your work. I had not gained by any written accounts so perfect an idea of what you were doing; and I assure you I am full of confidence that in this great work the Lord is your director. I find it a pleasure, whenever I find an opportunity, to speak in highest terms of the Richmond Institute and its most competent heads.

"S. F. SMITH."

The writer of the following letter, Rev. C. W. Waterhouse, for many years supported a pupil in the Richmond Institute, and in his will made provision by which a student would be supported in this School *for all time:*

"LAKEWOOD, OCEAN COUNTY, N. J.,
"December 5th, 1881.

"For ten years, while Mrs. Waterhouse was living, we supported a student in Richmond Institute, and I have continued it for two years since her death in August, 1879. Our first beneficiary named to us was Isaac P. Brockenton, now of Darlington County, South Carolina. (See page 79.) Of his labors and successes we have had very gratifying accounts in the Home Mission Monthly. * * * I have now passed my three score and ten, and I am no longer able to earn my living by labor; so that I shall probably need the interest money to use while I live. I cannot, therefore, now promise our usual yearly aid to a student at the Richmond Institute, however much I would delight in being able to do it uninterruptedly. But I rejoice in what has been accomplished, and I trust the good work will be continued uninterruptedly and faithfully by younger and stronger hands, both this and the following years, and after my decease.

"C. W. Waterhouse."

Dr. S. W. Field, who was a chaplain in the army and also a prominent pastor in New England, was always deeply interested in our work. In sending us a valuable collection of books from his library, he thus writes of his own struggles in securing his education, and refers to some of his experiences in the terrible days of the late war:

"Providence, R. I., January 25th, 1884.

"I left home when nineteen years of age, against my father's will, for Waterville College, then sixty miles from my native place, with six dollars in my pocket, not knowing where the next cent was coming from. By teaching winters and vacations, and practicing the most rigid economy, and teaching one term in the Academy after graduation, I entered Newton a term behind my class, and came out, after the three years' course, $400 in debt. And I would be willing to go through the same again, hard as it was, if I could begin life again.

There are sweets and advantages with all the bitterness of such, with love for Christ and your fellowmen to sustain you. Tell the men not to mind the hard rules, nor the practice of noble self-denial.

"A cigar never defiled my lips, so firm was I. Even in the army it was never a temptation. I met smoking, whiskey-drinking chaplains, and pitied them. Are any of your students from Fredericksburg? We had our hospital in the African Church, and their communion table was stained with our boys' blood. O, what a day that battle was! My clothes were wet with fresh human blood.

"S. W. FIELD."

On commencing the work in Richmond we found no records of any kind. There was no school furniture, no apparatus, no library, no course of study, and there was no one to give advice; many could not write their names, and all had but a very limited knowledge of the meaning of words. Modes of thought and of expression were entirely different on the part of teacher and pupil, respectively. Sometimes the teacher found it extremely difficult to convey his ideas. He had to explain what he meant to one of the most intelligent of the pupils, and *he* would convey the thought so as to be understood by all.

Our relations to the community in those early days were pleasant, and they have so continued until the present day. The pastors were cordial and friendly. Dr. A. E. Dickinson, then pastor of the Leigh Street Baptist Church, invited me to his pulpit and to his home. He has been a generous contributor to our work, and has served from the beginning on our Board of Trustees. The following letter, which is from the "Life of J. B. Jeter, by Dr. Hatcher," explains the interest Dr. Jeter ever manifested in our work:

RICHMOND THEOLOGICAL SEMINARY,<br>
RICHMOND, VA., March 20th, 1887.

*My Dear Dr. Hatcher:*

I learn with sincere pleasure that you are about to publish memorials of the late Dr. Jeter. I look forward to its perusal with peculiar interest. Dr. Jeter was a man for whom I had a most profound regard and a sincere affection. About nineteen years ago I came to Richmond an entire stranger. I was to succeed Rev. Nathaniel Colver, D. D., and Rev. Robert Ryland, D. D., in their work of training colored ministers. Our schoolroom was a small brick building, which stood in "the bottom," near Shockoe creek, below Broad Street, and was a part of the establishment known as Lumpkin's Jail. My own home was on the premises, in the house occupied by the former proprietor of the place, Mr. Lumpkin. Dr. Jeter was among the first to find his way to my unpretending home, in this most uninviting place, and to extend to me his sympathies, and to assure me of his hearty co-operation in my work. He and his "Junior," Rev. A. E. Dickinson, D. D., not only did what they could to make me feel at home, but tendered to me the columns of the *Religious Herald,* which they assured me would always be at my disposal in the interests of my work. Then, and ever afterwards, Dr. Jeter was a frequent and welcome visitor to our Institution. The young men always hailed with delight his coming, and listened to his words of instruction and encouragement with unfeigned pleasure. His attitude towards our work, both in public and private, largely contributed to secure, at an early day, the confidence and co-operation of the denomination in Virginia. His words of kind approval and appreciation to me personally were not only an encouragement, but an inspiration, as I felt myself honored in having so great and good a man for my personal friend.

So deeply had Dr. Jeter impressed his personality upon me, that whenever I saw his commanding form, whether he walked the streets or rode along on his old white horse, a benediction involuntarily escaped my lips. It was my privilege to join the company of mourners that followed him to his resting-place, on the banks of the James. And now, among the beautiful places where slumber the great and good in that "city of the silent," there is no spot near which I more reverently linger, than that where rest the mortal remains of Jeremiah Bell Jeter.

Chas H. Corey.

The Hon. J. L. M. Curry, ex-minister to Spain, has always been my personal friend, and also a friend and advocate of our work. The late H. K. Ellyson, one of the most distinguished Baptist laymen in Virginia, was a member of our Board of Trustees from the time of our organization as an Institution until his death. Dr. John William Jones, now of the University of Virginia, has contributed money and his talents to help build up our School. So have others in this city. From the day I entered Richmond, twenty-seven years ago, I have not seen a line in any of our papers against our work. Personally, my relations with the citizens have, ordinarily, been of the pleasantest kind. Occasionally an amusing incident occurred. One day in going down Franklin Street, just below the Capitol Square, I passed by a bar-room, in front of which several young men were standing. As I passed on I overheard one of them say: "That fellow preaches to the negroes." Assuming to be offended, I turned, and with feigned severity, demanded of them what they meant by insulting a gentleman in that manner. My business was to see Albert Brooks, a colored man who kept a liverystable near at hand. I incidentally pointed up the street towards the men in the course of my conversation, and they, suspecting that our talk was concerning them, the proprietor of the saloon and two or three more sauntered down to where we were. One of them, with an offended air, asked me what I meant by speaking to them as I did. I replied: "What did *you* mean by speaking to *me* as *you* did?" He replied: "O, we had no reference at all to *you!*" "What!" I replied, "Will you assure me, on your honor as gentlemen, that you had no reference whatever to me?" They solemnly asserted that they did not mean me at all. Then I replied: "If that be so, *I* should not have spoken to you as I did." The saloon-keeper said: "O, that's all right; won't you come in and take a drink?" I think that I would not have dared to assume so much indignation had not General Canby been in command of the city at that time. And I suppose the saloon-keeper, who was ever after a genial and cordial acquaintance, had fears that the "preacher to negroes" might have sufficient influence to get the military authorities to revoke his license.

April 27th, 1870, was bright and beautiful. Just before noon Uncle Jeffry came running to me where I was hearing my classes, saying, "the Capitol has fallen in." I thought but little of what he said, but seeing his excited condition, I hastened to the spot, and there was an appalling sight. The dead and dying were on the grass around the building, and there was a scene of indescribable terror and anguish. The Supreme Court of Appeals had assembled to decide upon the constitutionality of the "enabling act." Mr. George Chahoon was Military Mayor, and Mr. H. K. Ellyson had been elected by the City Council. The Court was to decide who was entitled to the Mayoralty, Chahoon or Ellyson. An immense concourse had gathered to ascertain the result. Everything was in readiness for the judges, when the ceiling and girders gave way, and "the mass of human beings who were in attendance were sent, mingled with bricks, mortar, splinters, beams, iron bars, desks and chairs, to the floor of the House of Delegates, and in a second more, fifty-seven souls were launched into eternity. The whole atmosphere was thick with a dense cloud of dust from the plastering, and the human beings sent up a groan which will ring forever in the ears upon which it fell."* About two hundred and fifty others were severely injured.

The bells tolled, crowds gathered. Wives, mothers and friends, wringing their hands, sought to find their loved ones. Hacks, ambulances, and all kinds of vehicles were there. On that sunny April day scenes were witnessed such as are unknown on battlefields, weeping women and children, walking among the dead and dying.

---

* See "*A Full Account of the Great Calamity,*" p. 13.

## CHAPTER X.

*The Freedmen's Bureau—Act of Incorporation—Purchase of a New Site—A Higher Theological School Needed—The Richmond Theological Seminary Incorporated.*

REFERENCE was made on page 87 to the Freedmen's Bureau. General O. O. Howard was Commissioner of this department of the government service, which had been called into existence by the exigencies of the times.

The late General S. C. Armstrong,* Principal of *The Hampton Normal and Agricultural Institute*, says: "General Howard and the Freedmen's Bureau did for the ex-slaves, from 1865 to 1870, a marvellous work, for which due credit has not been given; among other things, giving to their education an impulse and a foundation by granting three and a half millions of dollars for schoolhouses, salaries, etc., promoting the education of about a million colored children. The principal Negro educational institutions of to-day, then starting, were liberally aided at a time of vital need. Hampton received over $50,000 through General Howard for buildings and improvements."

\* See note C.

On page 88 it is stated that the Richmond Institute was chartered by the General Assembly of Virginia in 1876. The Act of incorporation is as follows:

## AN ACT

### To Incorporate the Richmond Institute in the City of Richmond.

*Whereas*, a lot of land with improvements, situate in the city of Richmond, has been conveyed by deed dated twenty-sixth January, eighteen hundred and seventy, to A. B. Capwell, James B. Simmons, Jay S. Backus, E. E. L. Taylor, Albert R. Brooks, Henry K. Ellyson, and R. M. Manly, trustees, and the survivors of them, upon the trusts that the said trustees should hold and apply the said land and improvements for the uses and purposes of an educational institution, and that the proceeds of the rental or sale thereof should be perpetually devoted to educational purposes as specified in said deed; and upon the further trust that the trustees or the survivors of them should apply to the General Assembly of Virginia for an act of incorporation, and when and as soon as a charter of incorporation is obtained creating and incorporating a literary institution or college, to be called the Richmond Institute, the trustees or their survivors should convey the property conveyed by said deed to the said corporation upon the trusts and conditions contained in the said deed; and whereas one of the said trustees, E. E. L. Taylor, has departed this life, and the other trustees above named have applied for a charter of incorporation, incorporating the following persons and their successors as such corporation, to whom said property is to be conveyed upon the trusts aforesaid: therefore,

1. *Be it enacted by the General Assembly*, That Nathan Bishop, Albert B. Capwell, Joseph B. Hoyt, William A. Cauldwell, Henry K. Ellyson, James H. Holmes, Richard Wells, Alfred E.

Dickinson, and Stephen Woodman, be and they are hereby constituted a body politic and corporate, by the name and style of The Richmond Institute, and by that name shall have perpetual succession and a common seal, may sue and be sued, plead and be impleaded, with power to purchase, receive and hold to them and their successors forever any lands, tenements, rents, goods and chattels, of what kind soever, which may be purchased by or be devised or given to them for the use of said literary institution or seminary of learning; and to lease, rent, sell, or ortherwise dispose of the same, in such manner as may seem most conducive to its interests; provided, that the lands, goods and chattels so authorized to be held shall not exceed in amount or value five hundred thousand dollars; and provided also, that not less than a majority of said trustees for the time being shall be sufficient to authorize the sale of any real estate belonging to said seminary of learning.

2. The said trustees and their successors shall have power to appoint a president, treasurer, librarian, professors and such other officers as they may deem proper; and to make and establish, from time to time, such by-laws, rules and regulations, not contrary to the laws of the state or of the United States, as they may judge proper for the good government of said seminary of learning. A majority of the trustees shall constitute a board for the transaction of business; and any vacancy or vacancies among the trustees, occasioned by death, resignation, or legal disability, shall be supplied by appointment of the board. The said trustees or their successors shall have power to increase their number to eleven if they desire to do so; and in that event they shall elect by vote of the board the persons necessary to make such eleven trustees. The said board of trustees shall have power to create an executive board, consisting of five of their number, which executive board (any three of them being present) shall have authority to transact all the ordinary business of the corporation, except the purchase or conveyance of real estate; the investment of funds; the appointment or removal of officers and teachers, and fixing their salaries; but the said board of trustees are

not required to create or appoint such executive board, unless they see fit to do so in their sound discretion.

3. The said seminary of learning is to be an educational institution, and the property owned by it, so long as the said corporation shall exist, is to be devoted to educational purposes as aforesaid.

4. The treasurer shall receive all moneys accruing to the said seminary of learning and property delivered to his care, and shall pay or deliver the same to the order of the board. Before he enters upon the discharge of his duties, he shall give bond with such security and in such penalty as the board may direct, made payable to the trustees for the time being and their successors, and conditioned for the faithful performance of his duty, under such rules and regulations as may be adopted by the board. And it shall be lawful for the said trustees, or for the Richmond Institute, suing in the name of such trustees or their successors, to obtain a judgment on such bond, or for any special delinquency incurred by said treasurer, on motion in any court of record in this commonwealth against said treasurer and his surety or sureties, his or their executors or administrators, upon giving ten days' notice of such motion.

5. The right is hereby reserved to the general assembly to modify or repeal this act at pleasure.

6. This act shall be in force from its passage.

## Richmond Institute Becomes a Higher Theological School.

In consequence of the increase of manufacturing establishments, and in view of other undesirable surroundings, it seemed advisable to secure a better location. After careful examination, on the 28th of June, 1880, the Trustees purchased of U. G. Hoyt, of Rochester, New York, for $5,000, nearly two and one-half acres of land on Reservoir and Beverly Streets, as a site for a new building. Reference to this transaction is made on page 103, in a letter written by Secretary Morehouse.

It soon became evident that the rapid increase of the colored population, and the phenomenal growth in the membership of the Baptist Churches created a necessity for a Theological School of a higher order somewhere in the South. The most thoughtful and judicious among both races saw that, for many reasons, it was desirable that the young ministers of the South should not incur the expenses of long journeys to Northern Seminaries, and that it would be better for them to be educated at home among their own people.

There was no distinctive Baptist school of the same aim and scope in the country nor in the world. The unprecedented openings for missionaries to Africa (which, for coming years, is to be the greatest mission field of the world) demanded such a school as this.

It was thought that Richmond, Virginia, was the place best suited for such an institution, as it is a great railroad center, and also an educational center, and the headquarters of the foreign mission organizations of the South.

A conference of nearly all the Presidents of the Schools of the American Baptist Home Mission Society was held at the Home Mission Rooms in New York, June 22d–24th, 1882. At this conference, after careful consideration, it was "Voted,

That, in their opinion, a higher Theological School ought to be developed at Richmond." Plans were subsequently laid and put into execution.

The following account of the action of the Trustees of Richmond Institute, and also of the Board of the Home Mission Society is taken from the January number of 1884 of the *Home Mission Monthly:*

"The annual meeting of the Board of Trustees of Richmond Institute was held at Richmond, Virginia, November 21st, 1883. There were present A. E. Dickinson, D. D., Rev. R. Wells, Rev. J. H. Holmes, and H. K. Ellyson, Esquire, of Richmond, and the Corresponding Secretary of the Home Mission Society. The meeting lasted about three hours, and was of a most harmonious and hopeful character. The most important action, which was taken after full discussion, is indicated by the following resolution, which was heartily and unanimously adopted:

*Resolved,* That, in the judgment of this Board, the time has arrived for the establishment of a distinctively Theological Institution of a higher order for the education of colored students for the ministry, and that Richmond is a suitable location for such an institution, and that we commend this subject to the renewed attention of the American Baptist Home Mission Society.

"At the meeting of the Board of the Home Mission Society, in December, 1883, renewed attention was given to this subject, and the following resolutions were adopted:

*Resolved,* That this Board hereby reaffirm their belief that the increasing intelligence of the colored people in America, and the need of well-qualified missionaries for Africa, imperatively demand that immediate measures be taken for the establishment of a distinctively Theological Institution at Richmond, Virginia, and that the Education Committee be, and are hereby authorized to make the necssary arrangements for the opening of the institution on this basis in the fall of 1884.

*Resolved,* That, inasmuch as this will require an increase in the number of instructors, and as this plan contemplates the permanent establishment of a theological institution that shall be for the colored Baptists what theological institutions in other sections are for their white brethren; and, inasmuch as the Society cannot well assume and continually bear the additional financial burden necessary to the execution of this design, *the Board do, therefore, earnestly appeal to men of wealth, who have at heart the welfare of the colored people here, and the evangelization of Africa, to do for this institution what has been done for others—namely, to endow two or more professorships in the sum of not less than twenty thousand dollars each.*

"It will be seen by the foregoing that a first-class theological seminary is to be established in Richmond in 1884. In the other institutions theological instruction will continue to be given for those who are unprepared, or for any other reason are unable to pursue a thorough course of study in the Seminary at Richmond. It is expected that the most advanced students from several institutions in the eastern Southern States will complete their theological course at Richmond.

"In addition to the regular course, a partial course will be provided, somewhat like that which is furnished in other similar institutions. We are sure that the means for this enterprise will not be lacking when the important bearings of it are clearly understood."

In carrying out the resolutions referred to above, application was made to the General Assembly of Virginia to change the name of the Institution. By acts approved February 5th and March 1st, 1886, the *Richmond Institute* became the RICHMOND THEOLOGICAL SEMINARY.

Through some oversight on the part of the Committee of the House of Delegates, who had charge of the bill, a mistake was made in the title, and it became necessary to pass another act to correct the error that had been made.

## AN ACT

*To amend an act entitled an act to incorporate the Richmond Theological Seminary, in the city of Richmond.*

Approved February 5, 1886.

1. Be it enacted by the general assembly of Virginia, That sections one, two, and four of an act entitled an act, to incorporate the Richmond Theological Seminary, in the city of Richmond, approved February tenth, eighteen hundred and seventy-six, be amended and re-enacted so as to read as follows:

SEC. 1. Be it enacted by the general assembly of Virginia, That H. L. Morehouse, Gardner R. Colby, Joseph B. Hoyt, William A. Cauldwell, Henry K. Ellyson, James H. Holmes, Richard Wells, and A. E. Dickinson (trustees), the successors of Nathan Bishop, Albert B. Capwell, Joseph B. Hoyt, William A. Cauldwell, Henry K. Ellyson, James H. Holmes, Richard Wells, Alfred E. Dickinson, and Stephen Woodman, which nine last persons were incorporated into a body politic and corporate by the act to which this is an amendment, by the name and style of the Richmond Institute, shall, as such successors, continue and be a body politic and corporate, and they and their successors, as such body politic and corporate, shall hereafter be known as the Richmond Theological Seminary, and by that name shall have perpetual succession and a common seal, may sue and be sued, plead and be impleaded, with power to purchase, receive and hold to them and their successors forever, any lands, tenements, rents, moneys, trust or endowment funds, goods and chattels of what kind soever, which may have been purchased by, or may have been or which shall be devised, bequeathed, or given to the said The Richmond Institute, or which may hereafter be purchased by, or be devised, bequeathed, or given to them, under the name of The Richmond Theological Seminary, for the use of the said literary institution or seminary of learning, and to lease or rent the same whenever most conducive to the interests of said institution, and to sell the same, whenever a majority of the corporators, who are hereby designated as trustees for the time being, shall authorize the sale; such authorization of sale to be made by a resolution in writing, after notice to each of the trustees then living that a meeting of them will be convened for the purpose of deciding whether such sale shall be made or not. The lands, goods, and chattels so authorized to be held shall not exceed in amount or value, at any one time, five hundred thousand dollars. The said corporators or trustees shall have no power to encumber by mortgage or trust deed the said property for any purpose whatever, and they are forbidden by this charter to use the principal of any endowment funds of the institution for its current expenses. The said corporators or trustees may vote by proxy or in person, as may be determined by them by a by-law to be spread upon the record of their proceedings, such by-law, when once adopted, not to be changed unless at least two-thirds of the then living trustees or corporators shall vote to change it.

Sec. 2. The said trustees or corporators, and their successors, shall have power to appoint a president, treasurer, librarian, professors, and such other officers as they may deem proper; to fix the term of office of all trustees, and provide for the election of their successors; and to make and establish, from time to time, such by-laws, rules and regulations, not contrary to the laws of Virginia, or of the United States, as they may deem proper for the good government of said seminary of learning. A majority of the trustees or corporators shall constitute a legal quorum or board for the transaction of business; and any vacancy or vacancies among the trustees or corporators, occasioned by death, resignation or legal disability, shall be supplied by appointment of the board. The said trustees or corporators, or their successors, shall have power to increase their number to eleven, if they desire to do so; and, in that event, they shall elect by vote of the board the persons necessary to make such eleven trustees or corporators. No person shall be eligible, as trustee or corporator, either to make such increase or to fill any vacancy in the trustees, occasioned by death or otherwise, unless he be a member in good standing of a regular Baptist church. The said trustees or corporators, or their successors, shall have power, if they see fit to do so, to create an executive board, consisting of five of their number, which executive board (any three of them being present) shall have authority to transact all the ordinary business of the corporation, except the purchase or conveyance of real estate, the investment of funds, the appointment of and removal of officers and teachers, or fixing the amount of their salaries. The trustees or corporators, or their successors, with the concurrence of the faculty of said seminary, shall have power to confer the degree of Bachelor of Divinity upon full course graduates of

REV. JAMES H. HOLMES,
Vice-President Board of Trustees of Richmond Theological Seminary.

the institution; and the honorary degree of Doctor of Divinity upon any person of suitable attainments, the concurrence of the faculty, in either case, to be spread upon the record of their proceedings.

Sec. 4. The treasurer shall receive all moneys accruing to the said seminary of learning and property delivered to his care, and shall pay or deliver the same to the order of the board. The treasurer, before entering upon the discharge of his duties as treasurer of the Richmond Theological Seminary, shall give bond, with such security and in such penalty as the board may direct, to be made payable to the trustees or corporators for the time being, and their successors, and conditioned for the faithful performance of his duty, under such rules and regulations as may be adopted by the board. And the said trustees or corporators, or their successors, or the Richmond Theological Seminary, suing in the name of such trustees or corporators, or their successors, may obtain judgment on such bond, or for any special delinquency of any treasury of the Richmond Theological Seminary, or on any bond heretofore given by any treasurer of the Richmond Institute, on motion in any court of record of the city of Richmond, against such treasurer and his surety or sureties, his or their executors or administrators, upon giving ten days' notice of such motion.

2. This act shall be in force from its passage.

J. BELL BIGGER,
*C. H. D. and K. of R. of Va.*

# AN ACT

*To amend an act approved February 5, 1886, entitled an act to amend an act to incorporate the Richmond Theological Seminary of the city of Richmond, and to amend the title thereof.*

Approved March 1st, 1886.

1. Be it enacted by the General Assembly of Virginia, That the title of the act approved February fifth, eighteen hundred and eighty-six, entitled "an act to amend an act entitled an act to incorporate the Richmond Theological Seminary of the city of Richmond," be so changed as to read "an act to amend an act entitled an act to incorporate the Richmond Institute in the city of Richmond."

2. That the words embodied in the first section of said act, approved February fifth, eighteen hundred and eighty-six, viz: "That sections one, two and four of an act entitled an act to incorporate the Richmond Theological Seminary, in the city of Richmond," be so changed as to read thus: "That sections one, two and four of an act entitled an act to incorporate the Richmond Institute, in the city of Richmond."

3. This act shall be in force from its passage.

J. BELL BIGGER,
C. H. D. and K. of R. of Va.

March 2, 1886.

## CHAPTER XI.

*Our Students—Results of Their Labor—Letters from Students.*

THE pupils of our School in its earlier history were not all ministers. Some were trained for teachers. For a short time young women were admitted to Richmond Institute (see pages 102, 103). From 1880, up to the time of the opening of the Hartshorn Memorial College in 1883, about thirty in all had been in attendance.

Many of our graduates became teachers, and others engaged in business. As financiers and accountants, some have no peers among their race. Ten of our former students have become physicians, and in their chosen profession some have already won distinction. Six have become foreign missionaries. Several are practicing law successfully, and others are editors of papers. Some of the graduates are in charge of institutions of learning, others are professors in such institutions. They may be found from Canada on the North, to British Honduras on the South; and from the great Northwest to the Atlantic.

It is quite impossible to estimate the vast amount of good that has been done by the students of this School, known successively as Colver Institute, the

Richmond Institute and the Richmond Theological Seminary.

But of the work done since the Institution has been under the care of the President, from 1868 until the close of the school-year, 1894, the follow- statements may be made:

| | |
|---|---:|
| In regular attendance from 1868–1894, | 766 |
| Attending Special Institute, 1868, | 81 |
| Attending Night Class of 1869, | 68 |
| Special Classes—Women, | 100 |
| Total, | 1,015 |

| | |
|---|---:|
| Total preparing for the Christian Ministry, | 530 |
| Total Graduates with Diplomas from Richmond Institute, | 73 |
| Total Graduates with Degree of B. D. from R. T. S., | 25 |

Fifty students who answered letters addressed to them report—

| | |
|---|---:|
| Churches organized, | 170 |
| Sunday-Schools established, | 270 |
| Persons Baptized, | 43,543 |

It is a conservative estimate to say that fully 100,000 persons have been baptized into the fellowship of Christian Churches by the 530 Ministerial Students who have attended the Institution.

## Letters From Students.

Among our earliest and most successful students was Sterling Gardner. After leaving the Colver Institute, he took the full course at Madison (now Colgate) University. While in the University he took several prizes, and was graduated with high honors. He was associate teacher in Colver Institute from 1872 to 1873, and from 1875 to 1876. At the earnest solicitation of Dr. Robert, of the Augusta Institute, at Augusta, Georgia, he was transferred from Richmond to that place, where he died December 8th, 1877. Dr. Robert expressed his profound grief at the loss his School had sustained, and writes, December 27th, 1877: "He was a most excellent Christian and a scholar of great promise." Miss Robert, describing the funeral, says: "Judge Gibson, his former owner, was there, and seemed much affected. He was so highly esteemed and loved in the Institute that he is greatly missed and regretted by father and all the students."

Rev. Henry E. Duers, of Sing Sing, New York, has organized four churches, planted four new Sunday-schools and baptized twenty-five converts.

Rev. M. S. G. Abbott, M. D., Pensacola, Florida, who was graduated from Richmond Institute in 1878, has organized five churches, ten Sunday-schools, and has baptized 230. Dr. Abbott, who graduated in medicine at Leonard Medical College,

Raleigh, North Carolina, has held important positions in Tennessee, West Virginia, and in Florida, in which places his ministerial life has been spent.

Rev. Richard Spiller, who left school in 1874, is pastor of the First Baptist Church, Hampton, Va., and Principal of the Spiller Academy. He has founded several churches and baptized one thousand eight hundred and seventeen persons. He has raised about ten thousand dollars for the building in which his congregation now worships. Elder Spiller holds important positions of trust and influence in the denomination, and is now President of the Alumni Association of the Richmond Theological Seminary. He is founder of the Spiller Academy, an efficient and growing institution. He writes, June 23d, 1894:

"I attribute my success largely to the training I received at the Richmond Institute, combined with the early training of my parents. The training I received in school has guided me all through my ministerial life, and it has a tendency to draw me nearer to the people, and has taught me how to become all things to all men that I might save some. God bless the School and its Faculty."

Rev. James H. Holmes has been pastor of the First African Baptist Church for about twenty-eight years. His church at one time contained the largest membership of any church in the world. He served the church and attended school at the same time. He left the Institution in 1874. He says, June 25th, 1894:

"I have married fourteen hundred couples, attended twenty-five hundred funerals and baptized about five thousand eight hundred people."

Rev. Charles H. McDaniel, Farmville, Virginia, has organized five churches, six Sunday-schools, baptized twelve hundred persons, and has built three church edifices. Rev. Mr. McDaniel has done much in quickening and building up the members of the churches. He says:

"The Seminary has made an everlasting impression on me, spiritually. It has prepared me, intellectually, for the duties of life, and has also enabled me to get nearer to my people. I have been called to sit in council to ordain six ministers and fifty deacons. I have taught in the Public Free Schools for nineteen years. I have preached about 2,000 sermons, and delivered 125 lectures. I have traveled on foot 24,700 miles, or nearly around the world."

Rev. Reuben Berkeley, Sassafras Post-office, Gloucester County, Virginia, has organized one church, seven Sunday-schools, and has baptized seventy persons, and has built one church edifice. He has taught Public Schools ever since leaving the Seminary. He says:

"The influence of the Seminary is constantly developing my spiritual life; it gives me daily strong command over self."

Rev. Richard Wells, for twenty-four years pastor of the Ebenezer Baptist Church, Richmond, Virginia, has been one of our Trustees since the founding of the School. For eleven years he was President of the Virginia Baptist State Convention, and has held other positions of importance of like dignity and responsibility. He has raised, from time to time, $16,600 to repair the beautiful edifice in which his people worship. He has baptized 3,801 persons. His connection with the Institute, as a student, terminated before 1875.

Rev. George W. Jackson, Brooklyn, Halifax County, Virginia, writes:

"I have helped organize five churches, have established four Sunday-schools, and have baptized 124. I am now Superintending Missionary Agent of the Halifax Educational Convention. I have been teaching in the Public Schools since 1875. The influence of the School upon my spiritual life stimulated me to become a model in my own life for those whom I instruct. It opened my blind eyes to see how limited my knowledge was, and created a longing, incessant desire for more knowledge."

Rev. J. B. Matthews, of Hixburg, Virginia, writes:

"I have organized four churches, and have paid the debts on two. I have baptized 2,500 persons. I have establishsd four Sunday-schools. My course in the Institution has done much both for my spiritual and intellectual life, and has drawn me closer to my people. I am very thankful to God. I owe all to Him and the Richmond Theological Seminary for my success in life. I will always feel very warm in my heart towards it."

Rev. Spotswood A. Anderson, who left school in its early history, has baptized 600 persons in the State of Mississippi, and sixty in the State of Virginia.

Rev. H. W. Dickerson, of Petersburg, Virginia, has organized two churches, established two Sunday-schools, built one church edifice and baptized seven hundred persons. He writes:

"My student career has enabled me to do my work better and has drawn me closer to my people."

Rev. William Cousins, of Martinsville, Virginia, writes, July 11th, 1893:

"I have been instrumental in organizing six churches. I have built one meeting-house and have baptized six hundred and three persons. I have established nine Sunday-schools."

Mr. Cousins was Principal of the Free School at Fincastle, Virginia, three years, and he has taught at other places in the State. He has been very useful as a missionary of the Virginia Baptist State Convention. He writes:

"The influence of the School has made me stronger as a Christian, and all that I am, intellectually, I owe to the School. My course of study has drawn me closer to the people."

Rev. I. P. Brockenton, A. M., has been for twenty-eight years pastor of the Macedonia Baptist Church, Darlington C. H., South Carolina. Taken in infancy from his parents, at twenty years of age he was sold to pay his master's debts. Securing the elements of an education, and enjoying the confidence to a rare degree of his owners under the old regime, he has a record of which any man might be proud. He taught the first school for Negro children in Darlington county. He has enjoyed the confidence of the community, and has held important positions in church and State. For a number of years he has been President of the Baptist Educational Misssonary and Sunday-school Convention of South Carolina, and Moderator of the Pedee Baptist Association. For eight years he was Trial Justice of Darlington county. He has been instrumental in organizing some fifty churches, and more than that number of Sunday-schools, and has baptized above three thousand persons. He writes:

"A large part of my success as a pastor is due to the influence which the Institute has had upon me.

I was there stimulated to strive to become 'a workman that needeth not to be ashamed.'"

Rev. W. W. Colley, of Winchester, Virginia, left school in 1875. He spent some eight years in Central Africa. He was born in 1854, and was graduated from the Richmond Institute in 1873. After a brief pastorate in Connecticut he went to the Valley of the Niger, in Western Africa, under the auspices of the Southern Baptist Convention, where he remained for five years. He was the first colored man to enter Africa as a missionary after the close of the war. Feeling the importance of organizing the colored people of America for work in Africa, he accepted an appointment of the Baptist Foreign Mission Convention of the United States, and labored for about three years under the auspices of that Society, which he had been largely instrumental in founding. He negotiated treaties with the African Kings while in the field, and did other valuable pioneer work in the cause of African missions. Brother Colley has, by his pen and his voice, done much to awaken and sustain an interest in the cause of missions among the churches at home. With health restored he hopes again to enter the Foreign Field. In speaking of the influence of the School upon his spiritual and intellectual life, he says:

"I there received those deep and powerful impressions which gave me the strongest missionary inclinations which have influenced me for more than twenty years. My intellectual life took its root in the influences and instructions of the Institution from which I went forth to the Master's work."

Rev. Nelson Jordan, pastor of the Mt. Shiloh and three other churches, attended the Richmond Institute in 1877, and has " ever since found use for the instruction there received, and the impressions received in the School will ever remain as graven images" before his sight. He has organized one church, two Sunday-schools, and has baptized one thousand and forty-nine.

Rev. Joseph Gregory, Franklin, Virginia, left school in 1878. He has organized twelve churches, built two, established four Sunday-schools and baptized two thousand five hundred persons. He writes:

" The influence of the Seminary on my spiritual and intellectual life has been good, and has drawn me closer to the people. I own a good home. I hope I stand well in the estimation of my neighbors, both white and colored. I have educated my son, who is now a practicing physican in New York."

Rev. J. S. Brown, pastor of Chestnut Grove Baptist Church, Bedford county, Virginia, was graduated from Richmond Institute in 1878. He has organized four churches, established ten Sunday-schools, and has baptized five hundred persons. He has built and paid for three churches. For ten years he has been Moderator of the Rock Fish Baptist Association. The Seminary has been of untold good to him.

Rev. Solomon Cosby, of Abeokuta, West Africa, was graduated from the Richmond Institute in 1878. He was sent out as a missionary by the colored Baptists of the South. He refers to his connection with the School as follows:

"None have been more blessed in that old building than myself. There I found Jesus precious to my soul. There I found loving Christian teachers who seemed to be never impatient in instructing me in the true principles of life as well as in letters, though stupid and indifferent as I was. When my prayers ascend for the Institute and teachers, and in my cherished recollections of Richmond Institute it will never be an easy thing for me to disassociate the old building on the corner of Nineteenth and Main Streets."

Rev. W. J. David (white) missionary of the Southern Baptist Convention, writes from Africa of Brother Cosby's death as follows:

BAPTIST MISSIONARY HOUSE,
LAGOS, W. C. A., May 3d, 1881.

*Rev. A. Binga, Jr., Manchester, Va.:*

DEAR BROTHER: It is my sad and painful duty

to inform you of the death of dear Brother Cosby, which occurred in Abeokuta, April 23d, at 12 noon, of jaundice fever. I only heard of his illness the day he died. When I received the letter informing me of his illness, I left at once for Abeokuta, hoping I might get there in time to minister unto him, and if he became able, to bring him to Lagos where he might have medical advice. I traveled during the day and the greater part of three nights, and walked the last ten miles of the journey that I might get there sooner. But you cannot imagine my feelings when I arrived and was told he "is dead and buried." Oh! my brother, you have heard those words at home, but never have they fallen upon your ear in a foreign land. You have never heard them where they meant that your only countryman and fellow-laborer was no more. You have never heard them when they meant that you were left "*alone*" in the midst of millions of heathen, with no friend, brother, and sympathizer. As I staid by his grave to strew flowers over it, I comprehended, for the first time in life, something of the meaning of the word "*alone.*" Only four months before I stood by the grave of my first born, at whose birth Brother Cosby rejoiced, and at whose death he mingled his tears with ours. These and the many other ways by which he endeared himself to us, caused my tears to fall at his grave. Your relations with him were doubtless more of an official nature. We revealed to each other our hopes and fears, our joys and sorrows. Therefore our loss is personal, and we have lost a brother beloved.

\* \* \* \* \* \* \* \* \* \*

He left us the 12th of March for Abeokuta; had been down on a business meeting. He had slight fevers while here, but was quite cheerful, and more anxious to return to Abeokuta than at any time before. He had become more attached to the place, and, besides, was preparing to build a chapel out of funds sent him by the Cosby Missionary Society of Richmond. When he landed at Abeokuta it was noon, and, as his journal says, " very hot;" yet he walked five miles to the mission house through the sun. This was highly imprudent, and resulted in a fever that same afternoon and night, and for several successive days. But they had stopped when he wrote me on March 29th. But I learned from his interpreter, cook, and others, also his journal, that after writing to me he began to have fevers every few days, until finally it resulted in jaundice fever, and he was confined to his bed only a few days. The Rev. Mr. Faulkner, the English Church Missionary, came to our mission and removed Brother Cosby to his home on Monday. At that time the symptoms were not serious, but by Wednesday they had so far increased that Mr. Faulkner sent a man to me, who was two days and a half coming. From Thursday till Saturday he was delirious at times, and in a stupor until his death. Even when aroused he did not speak unless questioned. Only one distinct sentence was heard from him. On the day of his death Mr. Faulkner said: "It may be the Lord's will for you to come to him and rest." He replied: "I want to go and rest with my Saviour." Shortly afterwards he obeyed the call of his Heavenly Master to come home and "rest from his labors." He was buried at 6 P. M., same day, by Rev. Mr. Faulkner, who nursed him like a brother, day and night, until his spirit took its flight. Mr. Faulkner deserves the profoundest gratitude of your Board. His post-office is Lagos. Your letter calling Brother Cosby home to rest came too late to be seen by him. I herewith return the bill you sent him.

I do not know whether you claim his diary, or his family, to whom I will write by this mail. If you desire any further information concerning him, let me know, and I will take pleasure in giving all I have or can obtain. I now close my sad duties. May all of us be as ready to go when the Lord calls as he was. He was *eminently pious*. Pray for us.

Yours affectionately,
W. J. DAVID.

Mrs. Nannie David, wife of Rev. W. J. David, writes of the same sad occurrence, April 30th, 1881:

"Many friends were present at his burial, and since the sad news reached this place, his friends, both foreign and native, are continually pouring in to sympathize with me and express their sorrow. Brother Cosby was much beloved by all—specially the young people. I need not mention the feelings of our hearts at this dispensation of Providence. He welcomed us upon our arrival, lived in the house with us more than seven months, rejoiced with us at the birth of our precious babe, mourned with us at her death, and in many ways endeared himself to us. *We* will miss him sadly, but for *him* we sorrow not. He has only laid down ' his sword for a harp; his cross for a crown.' "

Rev. W. M. Robinson, pastor of the Baptist Church, Fredericksburg, Virginia, left school in 1877. When called to the ministry he did not know a letter in the alphabet. During the year 1869 he walked eight miles three times a week to attend a free night school. His way was through the woods, and sometimes he became lost in the darkness. He writes, June 5th, 1894:

" In the same year I heard my old master reading in some of the Richmond papers that there was a school opened in Richmond for the purpose of granting young colored men an opportunity to study for the ministry. I wrote to the same, President Rev. Dr. Corey. I wrote on Sunday, and on Tuesday I received an answer to come to the School with a clear recommendation from any church. In 1872 I entered the Richmond Institute. I remained there five years. Since I left school I have organized twelve churches and thirty-three Sunday-schools. I have baptized 1,698 willing souls, and added them to the churches; these churches are all self supporting, have their own ministers and their own Sunday-schools. I am now pastor of two very fine churches, with a membership of 1,769 members. I have builded five meeting houses at a cost of $18,000, all of which are paid for except the one in this city, Fredericksburg."

Rev. T. J. Chick left Richmond Institute in 1879, and writes:

"I have been instrumental in organizing four churches and five Sunday-schools. Two of the Sunday-schools have since grown into churches. I have baptized sixty-three persons. Since leaving school I have been laboring as State Sunday-school Missionary for the American Baptist Publication Society for fourteen years; and I have been a member of the Board of Education and its treasurer ever since it was organized. I have held the position of first Vice-President of the Virginia Baptist State Convention for two consecutive years. I have found that an exemplary Christian life has much more influence upon the people than an eloquent tongue behind an immoral and unreliable life. I have been a diligent student—though constant and continuous travel has allowed little spare time, but that I have endeavored to employ wisely."

Rev. P. E. Anderson, Meherrin, Virginia, left Richmond Institute in 1879. He writes:

"I have organized one church, established six Sunday-schools and one Sunday-school Convention, composed of sixty-seven schools. I have baptized sixty persons."

Brother Anderson has spent much time in teaching, and has occupied various important positions in the educational and religious work of his portion of the State. He is pastor of two churches, New Bethel and Shiloh, and also President of the Bluestone Baptist Sunday-school Convention. "I owe," he says "many thanks to the Richmond Institute for spiritual and intellectual influences received. The Institute made me what I am, intellectually, morally and spiritually. From the Primary Old Field public schoolhouse I stepped into her walls, and was there encouraged to stand up for education, good morals and religion; since leaving the School, in 1879, I have never forsaken those principles. I own a small farm, horse, buggy and other property."

Rev. Aaron Wells, of Petersburg, Virginia, who left Richmond Institute in 1881, writes, May 20th, 1892:

"I have built three churches, established five Sunday-schools, and have baptized over one thousand persons. I took charge of the Wilborn Baptist Church, near Waverly, Virginia, in 1883, and resigned in 1888. I took charge of the Union Baptist Church, Yale, Virginia, 1888, and of the Jerusalem Baptist Church, Jarretts, Virginia, while a student in 1879. I am still pastor of the two last named churches. For several years I was Moderator of the Bethany Baptist Association, and President of the District Sunday-school Convention. The influence of the School upon my spiritual life was what the influence of devoted and religious parents would be to their children. At the School I also learned how to study. If my course of study has not drawn me closer to my people then I have made a great failure. But I have reason to believe that I have not made a failure."

Rev. Guy Powell, Franklin, Southampton county, Virginia, who left the Richmond Institute in 1880, has organized six Baptist Churches and eight Sunday-schools. He has baptized not less than 2,000 persons. He was Justice of the Peace in Franklin county more than three years; a member of the Senate of Virginia for four years, and a member of the House of Representatives two years. For seven years he has been Moderator of the Bethany Baptist Association, and is Chairman of the Bethany Baptist Sunday-school Convention. He has married about five hundred persons. He now presides over three churches, and preaches to 2,100 members. He writes, August 2d, 1893:

"The influence of the Seminary on my spiritual life has been great. The instruction received there has been the means of a great spiritual blessing, both to me and the people over whom I have presided for the last nineteen years. A desire for more knowledge was there created, and an impulse to search for hidden truths was there received. I have been drawn to my people by my course of study, and my people have learned to appreciate education when it is used in the right way."

Rev. Elisha Perry, Franklin, Virginia, who left Richmond Institute in 1881, has organized three churches, built three, established four Sunday-schools, and has baptized 180 persons. He writes:

"The instruction received in the Seminary has led me closer to the Saviour, and has helped me in trying to live in accordance with the divine law, and to be patient and long-forbearing. Save my conversion, it has had all to do with shaping the course of my spiritual life. Though I did not pursue my studies very far, I secured enough knowledge to steer my course, and to try to gather enough information to enable me to speak the Word as it is. I have been drawn closer to the people, and though I have spent the greater number of my days on earth, yet I feel that I am being blessed more and more."

Rev. J. H. A. Cyrus, who left Richmond Instutute

in 1881, is pastor of the Port Royal and three other Baptist Churches. He has organized one church, four Sunday-schools, and baptized 280 persons. He has been elected to various positions of responsibility, both ecclesiastical and civil. He writes:

"I remember with gratitude the few weeks I spent within the sacred walls of Richmond Institute. The noble Christian instructors there inspired me with an earnest purpose to work for Christ and the salvation of humanity. To this end I have dedicated my life. Intellectually, I received an incentive at the Institution which has kept me constantly striving to add to my knowledge, taxing every available means to this end."

Rev. L. A. Scruggs, A. M., M. D., Raleigh, North Carolina, who was graduated from the Richmond Institute in 1882, has organized two churches, built one church, paid one church debt, and established three Sunday-schools. Dr. Scruggs has been Professor of Physiology at Shaw University, and Resident Physician at Leonard Medical College Hospital. He is now Visiting Physician and Lecturer on Physiology and Hygiene at Saint Augustine's Normal and Collegiate Institute. He received the degree of A. B. and A. M. in course at Shaw University, and M. D. at Leonard Medical College. He writes:

"The influence of the Seminary has been most marked upon my life. I owe much (of the little I am) of what I am to the Institution, from a spiritual point of view. The influence upon my intellectual life has been also great. My course of study in the Richmond Institute has brought me in much closer sympathy with my people. I shall try, God helping me,.to make the very best of my life. I hope never to see the day when either Mr. P., my benefactor, or you will think less of me than you do now, but that you both shall feel that the time and money which have been spent to educate me have been well spent."

Rev. A. W. Pegues, A. M., Ph. D., Raleigh, North Carolina, was graduated from Richmond Institute in 1882. He has organized three churches since leaving school, established seventeen Sunday-schools, and has baptized 150 people. Dr. Pegues was, for five years, Professor of Latin and Philosophy in Shaw University, Raleigh, North Carolina, and is now General Sunday-School Missionary of the American Baptist Publication Society for North Carolina. He says:

"If I ever do anything in the intellectual world it will be due largely to the impressions made upon me at the Richmond Institute. My course has enabled me to reach the people as I never could have done without it."

Rev. C. S. Coleman, Scottsburg, Virginia, who left the Richmond Institute in 1882, writes, November 23rd, 1892:

"I have organized five churches, established two Sunday-schools, and have baptized 1,787 persons. The influence of the Institution on my life, spiritual and intellectual, has been alike good and great. The course of study seemed a strong cord to hold me to my people."

Rev. D. M. Pierce, A. M., who was graduated from Richmond Institute in 1882, Principal of Timmonsville (South Carolina) Colored Graded School, writes, February 3d, 1894:

"I feel deeply indebted to you as my benefactor and educational father. I have been busy from the day I left Richmond to this day, working for the civilization of my race. The people and the Lord have used me in their interest. I am still a student, and find my highest happiness in imparting the riches of Jesus to my unfortunate race. I can never forget you, who have settled my destiny for life and Heaven."

Rev. J. Milton Waldron, A. M., pastor of the Bethel Baptist Church, Jacksonville, Florida, and Professor of Rhetoric and Biblical Interpretation in the Florida Baptist Academy, was graduated from the Richmond Institute in 1882. Professor Waldron, from May, 1889, to September, 1890, was General Secretary of the Young Men's Christian Association, of Richmond, Virginia, during which time he secured $5,000 for running expenses and

PROF. J. E. JONES, D. D.

building, and assisted in starting six different Young Men's Christian Associations in as many different places. For more than two years Mr. Waldron was pastor of the Berean Baptist Church, Washington, D. C. He says:

"I was converted to Christ and led into the Christian ministry while in the Richmond Institute. Its spiritual influence has followed me and helped me most wonderfully."

Rev. C. H. Payne, D. D., Montgomery, West Virginia, was graduated from Richmond Institute in 1883. Dr. Payne writes:

"I am trying to do about three men's work. I am pastor of two churches, editor of a weekly newspaper, and deputy collector of internal revenue, and doing a large part of the work of superintending our State Mission work. I am often forced to work night and day in order to carry forward the many lines of work in which I am engaged."

In response to questions submitted he says:

"I have been instrumental in organizing eleven churches, establishing eight Sunday-schools, and have baptized 572 persons. I am President of the West Virginia Baptist State Convention."

Dr. Payne has held important positions of trust, both political and religious, and he says:

"The Seminary has exerted a helpful influence

upon my spiritual life such as only eternity can reveal. The development I have made intellectually is due almost wholly to the influence exerted by the Seminary. In proportion as my work proves efficient and helpful to my people, in the same proportion am I drawn to them."

Rev. J. H. Presley, who was cutting his three cords of wood per day in Virginia, and was unable to read or write when converted and called to the ministry, graduated from Richmond Institute. He entered the foreign field in 1883, and organized one Baptist Church in the Vey Tribe in Africa. He has baptized more than 100 persons. Since his return from Africa, in 1886, Brother Presley, after a pastorate of one year, has been engaged in Evangelistic work, as his health did not permit of his return to Africa. More than 2,500 have professed conversion in the various meetings conducted by him up to May, 1894. He writes:

"The influence of the Seminary on my spiritual life has enabled me to better understand my great responsibility to God and my duty to a lost world. In the School I learned how little I knew, and how much I am still to learn if I am to efficiently serve my Master and His people. I there learned to understand men, and thus I have been drawn to the people and the people to me."

Rev. J. J. Coles, Baptist Vey Mission, Manoh

Salijah, Sierra Leone, W. C. Africa, was graduated from the Richmond Institute in 1883. He commenced work in 1885; he had a day school and a Sunday-school. The material around him had to be grown before he could build. He baptized seven, and was instrumental in dispelling ignorance and superstition. His life abroad was an eventful one. Five times he was seemingly in the arms of death, and was only rescued by Divine mercy. He labored self-denyingly; and of suffering and hardship he had his share. He writes:

"When I came to the School I was a converted man, yet I had many false notions and imperfect ideas of religion. These were remedied by the instruction I received. There I dug up the old wooden foundations of ignorance, deeply mixed with superstition, and laid the corners with stone, on which I am still trying to build an edifice that will enable me to be more useful to my fellow men. My course of study draws me to my people."

On the 22d of July, 1893, Brother Coles returned to America for rest and recuperation. But zeal for the Master consumed him, and December 7th, 1893, "he fell on sleep," at the age of thirty-seven years. Devout men made great lamentation over him. He was a great man. He was beloved alike by his brethren at home and the natives of Africa among whom he labored, both young and old.

Rev. C. W. B. Gordon, pastor of the Tabernacle

Baptist Church, Petersburg, who left School in 1884, has organized one church, built two, and established a number of Sunday-schools. He says:

"I have baptized more than 1,500, am editor of the *National Pilot*, and am the author of a volume of select sermons. The influence of the Seminary on my life has been inestimable. It has been what fire is to the moving engine. I shall ever hold in grateful regard the Richmond Theological Seminary."

Rev. A. Chisholm, D. D., pastor of the Washington Street Baptist Church, Bedford City, Virginia, was graduated from the Seminary in 1884. He has been instrumental in organizing three churches and five Sunday-schools, and has baptized 700 persons. Dr. Chisholm writes:

"The Seminary was a source of inspiration to me. Never can I forget the glorious prayer-meetings enjoyed there. The influence of the Seminary upon my intellectual life has been strong, wholesome, and effective. My studies have drawn me closer to the people. I understand them better, and know how to reach their spiritual needs, and the same is true with respect to them; they can understand me better."

Rev. G. L. P. Taliaferro was graduated from Richmond Institute in 1885, and he is now pastor of the Holy Trinity Baptist Church, in Philadelphia. He has established one Sunday-school, and has paid about $5,000 on church debts. He has baptized about 300, and has had about 1,000 more converts in meetings he has held. He is Secretary of the Pennsylvania Baptist State Convention, and managing editor of the *Christian Banner*. He says:

"My Seminary course strengthened and more fully developed my spiritual powers. Intellectually, I owe the greatest part of my success to the Seminary. My course of study has drawn me to my people."

Brother Taliaferro has had great success as an evangelist, and as a worker and lecturer in the cause of temperance.

Rev. L. W. Wales, pastor of the Mt. Ararat Baptist Church, Williamsburg, Virginia, and the Rising Sun Baptist Church, York County, Virginia, was graduated from the Richmond Institute in 1885. He has organized one church since 1885, has raised for church building purposes, $3,000, has baptized more than 300 persons. He says:

"My course of study has enabled me to enter into sympathy with my people, and to labor cheerfully for their temporal and spiritual welfare. I have been able to save something for the 'rainy day.' I feel at a loss for words of praise in behalf of the School and the Faculty, for what they have done for me, and with a grateful heart I shall always pray for their success."

Rev. R. C. Quarles, pastor of the Pilgrim Baptist Church, St. Paul, Minnesota, entered school in 1880, and was graduated from the Richmond Institute in 1885. After successful pastorates in Farmville, Virginia, and in Buffalo, New York, he has entered upon an important field in the West. He has baptized 393 persons. He writes:

"The influence of the Seminary on my intellectual powers has been wonderful, having sharpened my reasoning faculties, and given me clearer views of the great doctrines of the Bible. It has set the wheels going, which in order to achieve success, must continue to go. My course of study has drawn me closer to the people, and has caused me to yearn for their up-building, intellectually, financially, morally, and spiritually, as never before."

Rev. Henry Madison, San Marino, Virginia, left school in 1886. He has organized two churches and five Sunday-schools. He has built and paid for four churches, and has baptized 1,428 persons, has married 112 couples, and has preached 346 funerals. His spiritual and intellectual life has been wonderfully quickened by his stay in the Seminary.

Rev. S. A. Garland, pastor of the Brookville Baptist Church, Amherst County, Virginia, since he left the Richmond Institute, in 1885, has organized two churches, four Sunday-schools, and has baptized 200 converts, and is President of the Ministerial Union, of Lynchburg, Virginia. He writes:

"If I am any good to the world, it is due to the training that I received in this School. I would have been in obscure life had it not been for the intellectual training that I received from the Richmond Institute. I can never forget your interpretation of the Acts of the Apostles. I have found that there is 'No royal road to success;' and I shall ever remember what you said to us, that we need not go through the world expecting the trees to bow down to us."

Rev. E. Payne, of the Fourth Baptist Church, Richmond, Virginia, writes:

"I have built one church and paid the debt on one church. I have baptized about 1,500 persons. I have had charge of but one church from June 1st, 1880, until the present time. I am a member of the Board of the Friends' Orphan Asylum, and a member of the Home and Foreign Mission Board of the Virginia Baptist State Convention. The influence of the Seminary has been very great, both on my spiritual and intellectual life. My course of study has drawn me closer to the people and has been of invaluable service to me. I am only too sorry that I have not been able to attend the School more."

Some additional facts in the life of Elder Payne,

who left the Seminary in 1887, may be of interest. The following statement is furnished by himself:

"I was working as a laborer for the city of Richmond when I was called of God to preach; but I knew not how, being in total ignorance. One day while working on the corporation I picked up a piece of a book on an ash heap. In this I saw a word, and other words just off from that. This caused me to like the piece of a book, and I kept it for two or three weeks, being ashamed to ask any one what it was. Finally I asked a fellow-workman, who laughed heartily at me for my ignorance, and told me that it was part of an old Dictionary. These pieces were dear to me and I held on to them. I took the notion to go to school, so I found a little girl about fourteen years old who was willing to teach me. I learned to spell and read very rapidly. So it fell on a day (Sunday) that I thought I might read a chapter in the Bible if I were to try. I told Mrs. Hannah Willis my wish. She told me if I could read a chapter in the Bible she would give me a Bible. She told me to turn to the 25th chapter of Matthew, as I would find that an easy one. But my trouble was to find Matthew, and then to find the chapter she named. I opened the book to what proved to be the 5th chapter of Revelation. This I read. She then gave the Bible to me, which turned out to be the half of one. I continued to go to school to anyone that I could, in the meantime working for an honest living whenever I could get work. When I took charge of this church, in 1880, I had these two pieces of books, a Bible, Dictionary, and a whole Bible. I had not a set of good books yet, but as I could, I bought books here and there."

Brother Payne for several years was a student at the Seminary, and serving the church at the same time. I secured a grant of books from the American Baptist Publication Society for Brother Payne, as I have for scores of ministers and students in the South. In the thirteen years of his pastorate he has built a substantial brick church, costing $30,000, on which there is no indebtedness. There are no rich members in the church, but all work for their daily bread.

Rev. A. R. Griggs, D. D., Dallas, Texas, who left Richmond Theological Seminary in 1887, writes as follows:

"I have organized ten churches, and built five. I have established about twenty Sunday-schools, and baptized about 100. As missionary pastor, I served Mt. Zion Church, Forney, Texas, from December, 1888, to 1889. I have held the following positions: Moderator of the Northwestern Baptist Association, Trustee of Bishop College and of Hearne Academy, President of the Baptist State Convention, State Sunday-school Evangelist, President of the Foreign Mission Convention of the

United States of America, member of the Advisory Council on Religious Congresses of the World's Congress Auxiliary, editor of the *Missionary Dollar Reporter*. The State University, of Kentucky, gave me the honorary degree of D. D. The influence of the Seminary kindled a flame of spiritual life in me that has enabled me to do my Christian work with a degree of joy, comfort, and understanding that could not have come to me otherwise. The spiritual life that pervades every department of the school work done in the Seminary, is so visibly manifested that no student, in my judgment, could escape its influence, so powerful yet pleasant. The Seminary's influence upon my intellectual life has wrought wonders for me in preparing my mind for systematic study and an appreciation for useful knowledge. The Seminary has given me a place among noble and intelligent people. Once I used to shun such company, or close contact with such men. Now I seek and enjoy it. I see the importance of intelligence, and long for it more and more. I feel that I have been able to serve my people better and more acceptably in the cause of Christ. My course of study has enabled me to reach my people in many ways that I knew not of before; therefore I feel myself drawn closer to them."

Rev. A. J. Brown, B. D., pastor of the Queen Street Baptist Church, Norfolk, Virginia, though but recently from the Seminary (1888), has done an important work. He has very materially reduced the heavy indebtedness of his church, and has baptized in all about 200 persons. For a young man, Brother Brown has held several responsible positions. For four years he was Secretary of the Home Mission Board of the Virginia State Baptist Convention, and in this capacity successfully carried on the mission work of the State.

Rev. Z. D. Lewis, B. D., a graduate from the Richmond Theological Seminary, in 1889, is pastor of the Second Baptist Church, Richmond, Virginia. On coming to this church as pastor, in March, 1889, he found it much in debt, with nothing in its treasury. All debts have been paid, and several hundred dollars are in hand for a new edifice. Pastor Lewis has baptized about 1,050 persons. He is Secretary of the Shiloh Association, and an officer in a number of important organizations. He writes:

"The influence of the Seminary has been such as to give me a clearer vision of my duty to myself, to my fellow-man, and to God, and its course of study and discipline have drawn and tied me to my people. The church evinces much love for the School, and confides much in its ability to furnish men for the times. The Lord has been with me, and greatly blessed me. Even now the future appears bright before me, with Him still at my right hand."

Rev. Forris J. Washington, Williamston, South

Carolina, left school in 1889. He has baptized sixty-five converts. He is trying to establish a school of high grade for the benefit of young men and women. In the years he has been teaching he has instructed nearly one hundred pupils. He writes:

"Words are not at my command to express the good effect of my Seminary course upon my spiritual and intellectual life. I regard the time spent in preparation for the Lord's work the most valuable time spent on earth."

Rev. P. S. Lewis, B. D., Salisbury, North Carolina, says:

"Since commencing my work here in 1889, I have paid one church debt and have baptized sixty. I am Moderator of the Rowan Association, and have held other ecclesiastical positions. The influence on my spiritual and intellectual life has been wonderful. I am still thirsty. Your friendly advice during my school life is to me a lasting treasure. May God prolong your days of usefulness to elevate my race."

Rev. Ellis Watts, B. D., pastor of the Harrison Street Baptist Church, Petersburg, Virginia, was graduated from the Richmond Institute in 1880, and from the Richmond Theological Seminary in 1890. He reports large congregations and constant additions. He writes:

"I have assisted in organizing five churches. I have organized five Sunday-schools and have baptized about 1,000. I was Missionary for the American Baptist Home Mission Society for nearly four years. I received the Degree of B. D. from the Richmond Theological Seminary. I entered the Richmond Institute in 1875 moneyless, and without friends able to help me. It was the friends of the Institution who helped me, and for this aid I can never cease to give thanks to God, for both my spiritual and intellectual life have been greatly helped by the Seminary. My course of study helps me to do better work with greater ease. By it I have been drawn decidedly nearer my people; their condition, their needs, and the way out, fill me with the greatest sympathy."

Rev. Z. Taylor Whiting, of Ordinary, Virginia, left school in 1890, and he has organized three churches, started three Sunday-schools, and has baptized 550 persons. He has also erected two church edifices. He reports:

"Spiritually, the influence of the Seminary has been a permanent guide, and intellectually, a helper in solving the hard problems of life. I cannot express the gratitude I feel for the help I received from the Seminary."

Rev. J. H. Turner, B. D., who was graduated from the Richmond Theological Seminary in 1890, writes:

"I have paid one church debt of ninety-five dollars. I have organized four churches and baptized eight persons. I am now State Sunday-school Missionary of the Virginia Baptist State Convention. I have held five religious institutes, and have received the Degree of B. D. The influence of the Seminary upon my spiritual life, by the contact with religious teachers and pupils, has been of untold value to me in my Christian experience. If I had not attended the Richmond Theological Seminary, or some similar school, principles and powers that were hidden would never have been developed in me. Theory and practice are drawing me nearer and nearer to fallen humanity."

Rev. E. V. Gassaway, B. D., pastor of the St. Paul's Baptist Church, Anderson Court House, South Carolina, since his graduation from the Richmond Theological Seminary, in 1890, has established twenty-five Sunday-schools, and has baptized 125 persons. He is President of the County Sunday-school Convention. He says:

"My intellectual aspirations have all been raised and improved by my Seminary life. I am only sorry that I did not get there earlier, and that I did not take a full college course. The Lord has greatly blessed me here, and I am very grateful for it."

Rev. C. G. Robinson, who was graduated from the Richmond Theological Seminary in 1891, writes from News Ferry, Virginia, December 15th, 1894:

"The Lord has helped me to do a great work here that shall ever remain in the hearts of the people. This has been done in a short time through much self-denial and sacrifice. The place is a new one, the people another people. My salary is small, but yet I live. I have baptized fifty persons since I left the Seminary."

Rev. P. H. Callaham, Society Hill, South Carolina, who was graduated from Richmond Theological Seminary in 1892, writes under date of March 9th:

"I have built two churches. I have baptized forty persons. My residence in the Seminary confirmed my faith in Jesus Christ, and inspired me with a constant search for knowledge. My Seminary course has drawn me much closer to the people. We have a school in connection with our church work. We are doing all that we can to push on the cause of Christ."

Rev. J. W. Boykin, pastor of the Baptist Church, Clarksville, Tennessee, was graduated in 1892 with the degree of B. D. He writes:

"The Seminary has been a great blessing to me in broadening my intellectual horizon. Spiritually, my idea of worship was greatly modified and improved. The School has brought me nearer to the people. I have baptized twenty-three."

Rev. S. W. Bacote was graduated in 1892 with

the degree of B. D. In August of the same year, he became pastor of the Second Baptist Church, Marion, Alabama. He has baptized about forty persons, and has paid off a church debt of $300. He became Principal of the Marion Baptist Academy in 1892. He was a member of the Advisory Council on Religious Congresses in connection with the World's Fair in 1893. He writes:

"My course of study at the Seminary has drawn me closer to the people, and has strengthened me both spiritually and intellectually."

Rev. W. T. Johnson, B. D., was graduated from the Richmond Theological Seminary in 1893. He writes, April 2d, 1894:

"Last fall I conducted a meeting here, and on the first Sunday in December I baptized ninety-seven, and there are others awaiting baptism. We are undertaking to build a new church to cost $9,000. The systematic training which I received at the Seminary in the line of work and study, has enabled me to have perfect control of my present situation. The influence of the Seminary upon my ministerial life is far beyond my comprehension or estimation. I am grateful to God, and to the President and Faculty of the Institution for the benefits that have come to me already."

## CHAPTER XII.

*Our Teachers—Sketches of Our Present Professors—Special Lectures—Occasional Lectures—Distinguished Visitors—Need of Endowment—Funds Secured—Attempted Removal.*

WE here give a list of the teachers from the commencement of the School until the present time.

### TEACHERS FROM 1867 TO 1895.

| | |
|---|---|
| Rev. Nathaniel Colver, D. D., President......... | 1867–1868 |
| Rev. Robert Ryland, D. D. Associate............. | 1867–1868 |
| Rev. C. H. Corey, A. M., D. D., President......... | 1868–.... |
| Miss H. W. Goodman, Associate.................. | 1868–1872 |
| Mr. Sterling Gardner, Associate................ | 1872–1873 |
| Rev. S. J. Neiley, A. M., Associate. ............. | 1873–1874 |
| Mr. Sterling Gardner, A. B., Associate.......... | 1875–1876 |
| Prof. George A. Minor, Musical Director......... | 1875–1881 |
| Rev. J. Endom Jones, A. M., D. D., Professor...... | 1876–.... |
| Rev. D. N. Vassar, A. M., D. D., Professor........ | 1877–.... |
| Miss J. J. Turpin, Associate...................... | 1880–1883 |
| Mrs. B. A. Clements, Musical Instructor.......... | 1881–1885 |
| Ernest Albert Corey, A. M., M. D., Professor..... | 1882–1885 |
| Miss Marie E. Anderson, Associate.............. | 1883–1884 |
| Rev. Nahum Hines, A. M. Professor.............. | 1884–1887 |
| Geo. R. Hovey, A. M., Professor.............. ..... | 1887–.... |

While they were students of the Institution, the following persons held commissions from the American Baptist Home Mission Society, as assistant teachers: Isaac T. Armistead, William Cousins, Joseph E. Jones, B. J. Medley, Andrew H. Cumber, Howard B. Bunts, Henry H. Johnson and Charles J. Daniel.

A number of other pupils have served acceptably as teachers, from time to time, being appointed for this service by the Faculty.

### Professor Joseph Endom Jones, D. D.

Joseph E. Jones was born of slave parents in the city of Lynchburg, Virginia, October 15th, 1850. He continued a slave until the surrender. Against the most earnest protestations of his mother he was put to work in a tobacco factory when he was not more than six years of age. At this particular period of the country's history the question of human slavery was agitating the minds of the people from Maine to the Gulf. The Southern States deemed it expedient to enact some very stringent laws with respect to the Negro. Therefore, the State of Virginia passed laws that prohibited anyone from teaching Negroes how to read and write, and if anyone was caught violating this law he would be imprisoned. The mother of Joseph believed with all her heart that the time would come when the colored people would be liberated. This idea so possessed her that she determined to have her son taught to read and write. She secured a man who was owned by the same family as herself to instruct her boy. This man came several nights each week to give him lessons. At this time—during the year 1864—things were in a desperate state in the South. Joseph's teacher soon began to think that he was running too much risk to give lessons at the boy's home, and he decided that it was not wise for him to continue. However, after some reflection, it was decided that the pupil should go once a week to the room of the teacher. The time fixed upon was Sunday morning, between the hours of ten and twelve. The white people usually spent this time at church, hence the selection. Later in the same year his mother secured the services of a sick Confederate soldier to teach him. The pay the teacher received was, something to eat. The instruction of this man was cut short by the surrender of General Lee. Immediately after the surrender, young Jones' mother placed him in a private school that had been opened by his first teacher, the late R. A. Perkins. When he commenced school after the surrender, his progress was very marked. He continued in this school two years. The most of the time he stood at the head of his class. The following winter he spent as a pupil in a private school taught by J. M. Gregory, now a Professor in Howard University, Washington, District of Columbia, and he was one of the best scholars in this school. In the spring of 1868, Joseph was baptized, and connected himself with the Court Street Baptist Church, of the city of Lynchburg, Virginia. October 6th,

1868, he entered the Colver Institute, now Richmond Theological Seminary, with a view of preparing himself for the Gospel Ministry. He spent three years here, taking the academic and theological studies then taught. April, 1871, he left Virginia for Hamilton, New York, and entered the preparatory department of Madison (now Colgate) University, from which he was graduated in June, 1872. The following fall he entered the university, and after a successful course of study, was graduated, June, 1876. The same year the American Baptist Home Mission Society, of New York, appointed him instructor in the Richmond Institute, and entrusted him with the branches of language and philosophy. In 1877, he was ordained to the ministry. In 1879, his *alma mater* conferred upon him the Degree of Master of Arts "in course." After Richmond Institute was changed to Richmond Theological Seminary, Professor Jones occupied the chair of Homiletics and Greek Testament. He is now Professor of Homiletics and English Interpretation. He not only performs well his work in the class-room, but takes an active part in all denominational movements, as well as other questions relating to the welfare of his people. He is a member of the Educational Board of the Virginia Baptist State Convention. November, 1883, Professor Jones was elected Corresponding Secretary of the Baptist Foreign Mission Convention of the United States of America. He served in this position until September, 1893. He was six years President of the Virginia Baptist State Sunday-School Convention. He has corresponded considerably for newspapers. He has had the pastoral care of a small church in the county of Chesterfield for about two years and a half. During this time he has baptized fifty persons. The Degree of Doctor of Divinity was conferred on him by Selma University.

The *Religious Herald*, of Richmond, Virginia, in speaking of the Professor, says: "Professor Jones is one of the most gifted colored men in America. Besides being Professor in Richmond Theological Seminary, he is Corresponding Secretary of the Baptist Foreign Mission Convention. He has the ear and heart of his people, and fills with distinction the high position to which his brethren North and South have called him."

In June, 1880, he was requested to speak before the American Baptist Home Mission Society at its anniversary at Saratoga, New York, on, "The Needs and Desire of the Colored People for these Schools."

The *Examiner*, of New York, in commenting on the address, said: "Mr. Jones is a young colored man, prepossessing in appearance and manners, and his address would have been creditable to any white graduate of any Northern college. It was sensible, witty, and eloquent."

A writer, in the *Baptist Encyclopædia*, says:

"Professor Jones is an efficient teacher, a popular and instructive preacher, and a forcible writer. In 1878 he held a newspaper controversy with the Roman Catholic Bishop Keane, of Richmond, in which the Bishop, in the estimation of many most competent to judge, was worsted."

Dr. William J. Simmons says: "In following the career of Professor Joseph Endom Jones, and observing and marking the changes in it, we can but say that it was simply marvelous. It must have been divinely ordered and superintended."

### Professor David Nathaniel Vassar, D. D.

The subject of this sketch was born in Bedford county, Virginia, December 5th, 1847. When three years of age he was stolen from his mother and sold into slavery, for he was born free. The man who did the deed was punished for his crime. He grew up in Lynchburg, Virginia, working at the barber's trade. He learned to read by studying the signs over the doors of the merchants of Lynchburg. In 1868 he entered the Colver Institute, and being an apt pupil, met with favor in the eyes of the teachers. In 1871 he attended the Academy of Madison University, and in 1877, he was graduated from the College Department with the Degree of B. A. When he graduated, he was at once chosen Professor of Natural Science and Mathematics in Richmond Institute, in recognition of his ability and learning. In 1880, Madison (now Colgate) University conferred on him the Degree of A. M. "in course." In the year 1892, Shaw University, of Raleigh, North Carolina, conferred upon him the honorary Degree of Doctor of Divinity. For thirteen years he has been pastor of the First Baptist Church, of Louisa, Virginia, and has there baptized 800 persons. He was elected Moderator of the Shiloh Baptist Association and served acceptably for two years. At present he is Treasurer of the Virginia Baptist State Convention, Treasurer of the National Foreign Mission Convention of the United States, and a trustee of Virginia Seminary.

The most important work of his life is his career as Professor of Biblical Introduction and Church History in the Richmond Theological Seminary, in which place he has left his impress upon the scores of students who have been under his instruction.

Professor Vassar is noted for his strong will, his exalted character, and his tender heart, and he is a great blessing to his race, and a worthy example to be followed.

## Professor George Rice Hovey, A. M.

Professor Hovey was born January 17th, 1860, at Newton Center, Massachusetts, an attractive suburb of Boston. He is of sturdy New England parentage. His father, Alvah Hovey, D. D., LL. D., is one of the most distinguished Baptist theologians, educators, and writers. His mother has been prominent in organizing and carrying on the

Woman's Baptist Foreign Missionary Society, a mission school, hospital work, and other good enterprises. Professor Hovey is the oldest of four children. He was educated in the public schools of Newton, and fitted for college at the Newton High School. He was graduated from Brown University in 1882, having, during his college course, enjoyed athletics as well as study. He took prizes in Latin and Greek, and was graduated with high honors. Entering Newton Theological Institute he was graduated in 1885, and spent a fourth year in post-graduate work. He served as acting pastor of the Baptist Church in Harrison, Maine, six months during the winter of 1886–7. For several summers he attended Professor W. R. Harper's Summer School of Hebrew as a student; and as an instructor at New Haven in 1885, and in Newton in 1886. He was married in 1890 to Miss Clara K. Brewer. He came to Richmond Theological Seminary in the fall of 1887. He has, while here, shown special interest in the library, raising above $3,000 as a fund for its use, and cataloging it by the most approved system. He has assisted in developing the high course of study now offered here, and especially in laying out the reading courses. For two years he did a large part of the editing of the *Seminary Monthly*. He has taken much interest in the work of the colored Young Men's Christian Association, instructing, weekly, a class of teachers in the Sunday-school lesson. His voice has often been heard

PROF. D. N. VASSAR, D. D.

in the temperance cause in the churches of the city. He is a frequent contributor to the columns of the *Watchman*. He also furnished a sermon for each of the two volumes on the Sunday-school lessons edited by President E. B. Andrews. His chief work, however, has been in his departments of Greek and Hebrew Interpretation, in which he tries to give courses fully equal to those in Northern seminaries. Professor Hovey is an enthusiastic and conscientious teacher. His abilities as a scholar and writer command the respect of his acquaintances; and he is justly entitled to the high esteem in which he is held by all.

In order to carry out more fully the design of the patrons of the Institution, special courses of lectures have been delivered to the students on subjects pertaining to the work of the ministry, from time to time. These lecturers have been: Marsena Stone, D. D., formerly Professor in Dennison University; W. W. Everts, D. D., Chicago, Illinois; Alvah Hovey, D. D., LL.D., President of Newton Theological Institution, and E. G. Robinson, D. D., LL.D., formerly President of Rochester Theological Seminary, and subsequently President of Brown University.

In addition to these courses of lectures, distinguished men in our city, and noted preachers from various parts of this country and from abroad, have favored our students with highly instructive and profitable discourses. The brief addresses of the distinguished Dean Howson, of Chester, England, and of Dr. Henry Grattan Guinness, of London, will never be forgotten.

We have had visits from distinguished statesmen of our own country, of Canada and of Great Britain.

The importance of securing an endowment was recognized by the friends of the School at an early day. To them it seemed to be an *endowment* or *death*. Dr. T. J. Conant, the distinguished Biblical translator, in writing to a friend, gives his experience:

"I have spent thirty-two years in the service of our denomination, as a teacher in its colleges and theological seminaries. My salary after the first two years was never sufficient to cover the very moderate expenses of my household. I seldom knew the luxury of freedom from debt. During those thirty-two years, more than twenty thousand dollars of money, which came to me from my father, was thus expended in the struggle to sustain my family, in the service of an unendowed institution."

Our students, in order to show their interest in securing an endowment, paid more than $1,000 towards it.

It is stated on page 36 that Dr. Lathrop and J. B. Hoyt visited Charleston, South Carolina, in 1865; and on page 104, is an account of an interview with the latter, at his home, in 1884. Secre-

RICHMOND THEOLOGICAL SEMINARY. 183

tary H. L. Morehouse, on the same page, states what followed.

We have now the following PROFESSORSHIPS and SCHOLARSHIPS fully or partially endowed:

| | |
|---|---:|
| THE J. B. HOYT FUND, Chair of Church History, | $25,000 00 |
| THE JOHN D. ROCKEFELLER FUND, Chair of Biblical Theology, | 25,000 00 |
| THE UNION PROFESSORSHIP, Chair of Biblical Interpretation, | 6,917 41 |

### SCHOLARSHIPS.

The following "Funds" have been established, and the income from them is to be used in helping needy students:

| | |
|---|---:|
| The Emily C. S. Colby Fund, | $ 500 00 |
| The Susan C. Reed Scholarship, Established by Dr. N. Colver's daughter, | 1,000 00 |
| Ths Rev. C. W. Waterhouse Scholarship, | 1,000 00 |
| The Lydia S. Tolman Fund, In Memory of Mrs. Lydia S. Tolman, Lynn, Mass., | 1,400 00 |

### LIBRARY FUND.

This Fund now amounts to $3,120 50.

In addition to this there is available the income of $1,000, until such time as the principal may be needed for its designated purpose.

The BUILDING FUND is $12,669.24 in cash, and ten shares of railroad stock.

### The D. Henry Sheldon Loan Fund.

This fund of $100 is given that it may be lent temporarily to needy students.

In 1894 a suggestion was made that it might be desirable to remove the Seminary to Atlanta, Georgia. Some very strong reasons were urged in favor of such a course. The matter was very thoroughly discussed by the friends of theological education. While the discussion was thorough and exhaustive on both sides, it was conducted in the most friendly manner, the desire of all being to ascertain what, upon the whole, was best for the colored Baptists of the South. It was decided, however, that it would be both unwise and impracticable to undertake to remove the Seminary from Virginia. The Corresponding Secretary of the American Baptist Home Mission Society, Dr. T. J. Morgan, writes, December 11th, 1894:

"I think that no further steps will be taken at all looking to the removal; that matter may be regarded as settled. * * * * We have found that it is impossible to move the Seminary."

## CHAPTER XIII.

*The Old African Church—A Historic Building—Its Religious History—Dr. Ryland's Pastorate—Pastorate of Rev. James H. Holmes.*

AS the first work in Richmond for colored preachers was commenced in the old African Church, and as it was so intimately connected with much of the past history, both of the white and colored people of the city, it seems desirable to devote a chapter to it.

The Richmond *Dispatch*, of August, 1876, contained a number of interesting letters pertaining to the building. From these letters, which were afterwards published in pamphlet form, copious extracts will be made.

In 1802 the First Baptist Church erected a house of worship at the northeast corner of H or Broad and College Streets. Originally the building was about forty by forty feet. Subsequently it was enlarged on three sides, making a cruciform building one hundred feet by seventy. The Richmond *Dispatch*, about the time the old building was torn down, in 1876, published the articles to which reference has been made, and says:

"The OLD CHURCH has been for many years a land-mark, and in the minds of our people is associated with happy memories of by-gone days, and of customs that have been swept away by the tide of years and results of the war. When its foundation was dug and its corner-stone laid, Richmond was but a country town. Its streets were poorly graded, and only in a few instances paved. Where now is the fashionable and brilliant West End was then a forest.

"Main Street, in the neighborhood of the Old Market, monopolized much of the business of the place, while the upper part of the street and Broad Street were just beginning to claim some attention by stores being erected here and there upon them.

"The Baptists, now a denomination of immense number in the State, were then few and by no means possessed of the influence they now enjoy. The old church soon became too small for their needs, and was passed into the hands of trustees for the benefit of the colored people of that denomination. In slave times the congregations were always large. Of the happy and peaceful looking flocks that gathered there in those days; of the content that sat upon their countenances; and of their comfortable appearance and respectful demeanor, the writer of Virginia history will have occasion to speak. In the old church worshipped congregations of immense size, and their sacred songs were ever an attraction, while their fervid piety and earnest exhibition of religious feeling were marked with all the characteristics of the race.

"In the scarcity of public halls the church was often used for public meetings. Democrats and Whigs held conventions and had rallies there. The old walls, now soon to mingle with the dust, have echoed the eloquence of some of the foremost orators that Virginia ever produced.

"In the last days of the Confederacy, when starvation and battle were weakening Lee's army; when the smoke from the enemy's guns was daily wafted into the city, and when despair was seizing the people, a grand mass-meeting was called at the African Church, and the voices of Jefferson Davis, Judah P. Benjamin, and other orators aroused new zeal and inspired fresh hope in the struggle, and helped to postpone, for a time, the inevitable hour of surrender. \* \* \* \* \* \* \*

"As a place of entertainment and interest, we may say that the old African Church had no equal. Every Northerner who came to see Richmond and its many features of interest and historic note, as a matter of course, visited the old church. Before the war the singing there was remarkably fine, and Sunday was generally selected for the visit.

"As a place of amusement, too, it has some notoriety. Ole Bull charmed hundreds of Richmond people in days gone by, and it was there that Tom Thumb was greeted when he first commenced coming to Richmond. Blind Tom, too, we believe, gave some of his performances in the same building, both during and after the war. Our citizens will also remember with delight that they heard Patti, Sontag and Parodi here, and it was with no little delight that the writer heard Paul Julien play the "Carnival of Venice" on one string, a few years after the signing of the Declaration, within these classic walls."

Among a few of the notable men who addressed vast auditories from the platform of this historic building, may be mentioned the following:

"Governor William Smith, Benjamin Watkins Leigh, John Minor Botts, Henry A. Wise, Tim. Rives, John Letcher, Roger A. Pryor, William C. Rives, R. M. T. Hunter, Geo. W. Randolph, Judah P. Benjamin, Jefferson Davis, Patrick Henry Aylett, John Tyler, Briscoe G. Baldwin, and John B. Baldwin. * * * * * * * *

"Not least among the historic reminiscences of this old building is the famous meeting that took place in 1864, just after the noted peace conference at Fortress Monroe. Our people did not know how sick they were; the soldiers, though starving, were dreaming of better rations for the future, and our cause was generally lacking of that vitality that betokens success. One of the grandest meetings ever held in Richmond was held in the church.

"Stirring addresses were delivered by President Davis, Judah P. Benjamin, and other notables, which led many of our staid citizens to invest much of their earnings in Confederate States bonds, and many of our ladies to put down on the platform their much-cherished jewels. It was a scene well worthy of the worn traditions of Sparta, for many of our ladies took off their breast-pins and bracelets and deposited them upon the table before the speaker. This was the last meeting ever held in Richmond under Confederate auspices."

From the Richmond *Dispatch* of August 17th, 1876, we have the following:

"When the war was about fairly commenced, a number of persons from the Cockade City came over to Richmond, and headed by General Roger A. Pyor, they went to the old church, where an improvised meeting was held. The church was soon thronged. The Petersburgers had the 'stars and bars' at the head of their column, and this was probably the first occasion upon which the Confederate flag was displayed in Richmond. It was upon that memorable night that Pryor fairly fired the Southern heart with his great speech. Many persons who bitterly opposed even the thought of war were changed in sentiment, and the meeting soon became one of the wildest enthusiasm. John Minor Botts was holding forth the same night at the old Metropolitan Hall, and it was upon that occasion that Mr. Botts predicted in his speech what afterwards came true concerning the war.

"The reputation of many local orators was formed in the African Church. Colonel Marmaduke Johnson and Colonel Thomas P. August frequently spoke there. But what we started to write was that E. Z. C. Judson, *alias* Ned Buntline, thundered in the old church in behalf of the American Order, which was the prelude to the 'Know-Nothings.'

"It is stated upon good authority that when the old theatre was destroyed by fire in 1811, the African Church was used as a receptacle for the dead and wounded. The negroes assembled at the church, and sang and prayed during the fire, and they claimed that their church was saved from destruction by their prayers.

"The prices paid for the hire of the building were sometimes high. The first year of the war, and even before that time, it was not an uncommon thing for twenty-five dollars to be paid for the use of the house just for one night."

A correspondent in the Richmond *Dispatch*, of the 17th of August, 1876, contributes the following:

"During the winter of 1864, one of Lee's veterans, from the rural districts, who had been imbibing rather freely of apple-jack ($20 per canteen, Confederate currency), chanced to be in the city, 'running the blockade' from the home-guard pickets. On his way back to camp he strolled into the African Church for the sake of getting warm, and comfortably seated himself in a pew convenient to the stove. One of the elder brethren was exhorting the congregation at the time from the parable in Scripture where the sheep and the goats were prominent in his argument. He was portraying in vivid language the terrors of the great judgment-day, and impressing upon his hearers that the saved would be among the sheep and the lost among the goats. 'On dat day, dear breddern,' said he, 'de sheep will be on de one side and de goats on de udder, and I piously hopes dere will be lots of sheep from this fold. But,' with a pause for effect, 'who will be de goat?' After an impressive pause he repeated in louder tones: 'I say, breddern, on dat great day *who'll be de goat?*' Another impressive pause and silence everywhere. About this time the old Confederate began to rustle about in his seat, and simultaneously the ominous voice came from the pulpit, '*Who'll be de goat?*' The imbibing rebel, drawing himself up as straight as he could from his seat, shouted out, 'See here—hic—mister, sooner than see—hic—this thing play out—hic—I'LL BE DE GOAT.' The effect of this unexpected response is left to the imagination of the reader. \* \* \* \* \* \* \* \*

"No scene of transformation could be more complete than that presented within the walls of this old and historic building since the war. We had seen during those dark days such men as Davis, Toombs, Yancey, Benjamin, and others, 'firing the Southern heart,' and when the smoke of the battle had cleared away what was to be seen? an assemblage of our former slaves—the first ever held in the South. They had been invested with all the rights of citizenship, and spoke with an assurance that would indicate that they had owned the land since the days of their birth. Among the men who spoke to them in their gatherings were Horace Greeley, Gerritt Smith, Henry Wilson, General O. O. Howard, Judge Underwood, and others whose names are prominent in the history of Southern reconstruction."

George W. Smith says in the *Dispatch* of August 18th, 1876:

"Allow me space in your columns to make an addendum to the history of the old African Church, which appeared in yesterday's *Dispatch*—viz: That at an early day of the month of April, 1861, the largest meeting ever held in that church took place in behalf of the Union, the Constitution, and the Enforcement of the Laws.

"I had the honor to preside at that meeting. Such men as Waitman T. Willey, of Monongahela county; John A. Campbell, of Washington county; and the late Geo. W. Summers, of Kanawha county—all of them being members of the State Convention or of the Legislature, both bodies then being in session in this city—made able and eloquent addresses to the large audience in behalf of the Union."

In the year 1841 the white people built a new

church on the corner of Twelfth and Broad Streets. Dr. Robert Ryland, then connected with Richmond College, took pastoral charge of the colored church, in 1841. The church paid him a salary of $500 per annum. I am indebted to an address delivered by Dr. Ryland at the celebration of the the close of the first century of the First Baptist Church, for some interesting statements. He says:

"The colored brethren were informed that they could occupy the old house as soon as it should be vacated by the whites, and that, on their payment of $4,500, which they thought they could raise, the property should be deeded to trustees, to be held by them for the *exclusive and perpetual use* of the First African Church. Both these pledges were redeemed, and in the year 1849 the property was conveyed to its present incumbents, who had paid $5,000.19, principal and interest. \* \* \*

"It had long been the habit of many of the attendants to come late to meeting. This habit was not only hurtful to those who indulged it, but it disturbed the quietness of the audience and interrupted the preaching. At first the pastor thought that the employers might have detained their house servants so long, as to prevent their reaching the sanctuary in time. On inquiry, he found that most of the families who permitted their servants to come at all, allowed them ample time to secure punctuality. He found, moreover, that when there was a marriage to be solemnized, or something amusing to be exhibited, everybody was in time. After trying by moral suasion, very urgently, but in vain for several years, to break up this annoyance, he induced the deacons to pass an order that the church-yard gates should be locked forty-five minutes after the time to begin worship, so as to exclude incomers after the sermon began. This measure seemed harsh, but its effect was most salutary. Very few were really kept out, and loiterers were taught a valuable lesson. The evil being, to a great degree corrected, the rule was, after six months, suspended.   \*   \*   \*   \*   \*   \*

"There were usually at our College some twenty or twenty-five young men, studying for the ministry. And, like theologians, generally, most of them were not burdened with money. Partly to help their pockets and partly to improve their gifts, as well as to get assistance in his arduous work, the pastor often invited these young men to officiate for him in the afternoon. At the close of a sermon by one of these, Deacon Simms, an excellent man, was requested to follow with prayer. He offered up a devout petition to God for His blessing on the truths just delivered, and for large grace 'on our stripling young brother that is trying to learn how to preach.'

"The good order of the congregation was remarkable—for its size, it was wonderful. During the twenty-four years of his ministry among them, the pastor did not see a single instance of a group of persons, young or old, engaged in talking and laughing during public worship. \* \* \*

"It is a misconception of the African race, which many Anglo-Saxons cherish, *that all negroes are alike.* While the whole human family are depraved, and the sameness of condition, surrounding a particular tribe, will impress on it a peculiar type of character, still there is as much *individuality*—as much variety of intellectual and moral temperament—among the negroes as there is among persons of any other race. I have witnessed as bright examples of godliness, of disinterested kindness, of real gentility of manner, and of native mental shrewdness among them as among other people. Many of the old men and matrons were brought up in the best families, and understood all the proprieties of life. Their manners were polished, and their principles correct. This, to a partial extent, was true of some of the young people of both sexes. Say you this was the result of imitation? Very well. And do not *our* children get all their refinement by imitation? \* \* \* \* \* \* \*

"One of my members went on a certain occasion to hear a learned gentleman, then a pastor of this city. I do not vouch for the justness of the criticism, but, being asked how he liked the sermon, he said: 'He preaches too much out of the dictionary.'

"From October 1st, 1841, to July 1st, 1865, the additions by baptism to the First African Church were 3,832. Of this number no larger a proportion fell away from the belief and practice of the truth, than is usual in our average churches."

It may be interesting to know that the Richmond Missionary Society was formed in the year 1815, in this church, with the sole purpose of sending missionaries to Africa. In January, 1821, Lott Carey and Colin Teague, members of this church, sailed with a number of colonists for Africa. In the absence of the Governor of Liberia, the entire government of the colony devolved on Lott Carey. He was considered one of the most gifted colored men of his time.

The present pastor of the church is Rev. James H. Holmes. When he took charge of the church in August, 1867, the membership was about 4,000. In 1870, it numbered 4,683. During 1870–71, the names of 2,200 persons who failed to respond to a call for a new enrollment, were dropped. There were left 2,400 in 1871. In the great revival of 1878 the writer was present, and saw the pastor immerse 598 in three hours. Again in June, 1894, the pastor immersed 245 in one hour. During the twenty-eight years of Mr. Holmes' pastorate, he has baptized nearly 6,000 persons. On one occasion more than a thousand went out and formed a new church.

Rev. Mr. Holmes was a pupil in the School in its early history. He could be seen daily going along the streets of the city with his books under his arm, though at that time he was pastor of the largest Protestant Church in the world. He and Rev. Richard Wells, the beloved pastor of the Ebenezer Baptist Church, and later Rev. Evans Payne, the more youthful, but equally energetic pastor of the Fourth Baptist Church, for several years were earnest students in the Institution, though each had a large church, numbering many hundreds, under his care. Brother Holmes often refers to an occasion under the old regime, when he, as a violator of the law, had to suffer its extreme penalty. One of the city ordinances made it unlawful for more than five colored people to be assembled without the presence of a white man. One Sunday morning, instead of going home from prayer-meeting, he attended a wedding breakfast, at the earnest entreaty of his wife. While engaged in the enjoyment of the meal the officers of the law came upon them, and they were all arrested. On the following morning he was publicly flogged in due and approved form, and his wife was fined five dollars. Mr. Holmes thinks this another instance in which a woman's influence led to a man's humiliation.

The cost of the new church edifice built by Pastor Holmes and his people was $35,000.

## CHAPTER XIV.

*The Slave as a Man—As a Christian—As a Soldier—
As a Free Man—Statistics.*

THE writer was not acquainted with the colored man as a slave. But he has heard much of the fidelity of slaves to their masters, and of the regard in which some were held by their old owners. Dr. John A. Broadus, in his Commentary on the Gospel of Matthew, says: "A 'Confederate' officer and the slave who attended him in camp would often risk their lives for each other, while his other slaves at home took the most faithful care of his wife and his children."

It will remain always to the praise of the colored man that he was true and faithful to the family of his master when he was in the army fighting for a cause which, if successful, would perpetuate his bondage. In conversing with scores of people during thirty years, I have never heard of an instance of betrayal of trust on the part of a slave. Confederate generals, doctors, lawyers, and ministers, and private citizens give their unanimous testimony that the slaves toiled industriously, and faithfully cared for the unprotected women and children who were left in their charge. This faithfulness on the part of the slave has filled the English-speaking race with surprise and admiration.

A Southern minister says: " In a county sometimes 12,000 out of 15,000 were black people. What a blow they could have struck! During all the years of that dark war did these black men ever lift their hand in one revengeful act? Can you point to one single instance of revenge? Did not they protect the interests of their masters during the war?"

A volume might be written, giving instances of affectionate devotion to their old masters, and of sublime faith in God who they believed was fighting their battles for them. The following incident is taken from the *American Missionary* for 1894, page 19:

" During the last days of the civil war a Confederate soldier lay dying on a Virginia battle-field. His faithful slave valet stood at his side. As the master was breathing his last he said to the slave: ' Go, go.' ' Go where, master?' asked the slave. ' Go North and be free. You are too noble a man to be a slave.' ' No, master, I'se obliged to go back. I promised missus that if you fell I would bring back to her the Bible she sewed in your vest pocket. I would like to be free, but I'se obliged to go back.' The master died. Back the slave went, across rivers, over plains, through cane brakes, till he reached the old Mississippi plantation. When he had delivered the book he was remanded to slavery."

The following is from the *Christian Herald:*

"Near the Black Mingo Baptist Church in Georgetown District, South Carolina, among the tombstones which mark, and will ever make the spot dear to all who may visit the place, one may read the following on a marble slab:

Sacred to the memory of

"BILL,"

A Strictly Honest and Faithful Servant of

CLELAND BELIU.

"Bill was often entrusted with the care of personal merchandise, to the value of many thousand dollars, without loss or damage.

"He died on the 7th day of October, 1854, in the thirty-fifth year of his age, and an approved member of the 'Black Mingo Baptist Church,' of which his master was a deacon. 'Well done thou good and faithful servant, enter thou into the joy of thy Lord.' Erected by his master.—C. B.

"This is one of a thousand evidences of affection held in ante-bellum days for faithful servants by their masters.

—W. H. ROBERT, *an ex-Slave-Holder.*"

Rev. Dr. Allen, brought up in the South, a slaveholder's son, says:

"I have carried in my heart since I was a boy,

a prayer of an old colored man whom my father owned. As I came up one evening, near the fence, I heard a strange noise. I stopped—I was a little frightened. I soon found the old colored man was there, engaged in prayer near the fence. I heard him pray to God to wash his soul in the blood of Jesus, to clothe him in Christ's righteousness, and towards the close of his prayer, he said: 'Now, Lord, bless the corn-fields and the old people at the house, and God bless old master's little boys.' When I heard that, I felt like going down on my knees beside him, for I felt that I stood on holy ground. The heart of that man reaching up to Him who could bless the little boy! We saw him die in a few months after. And, brethren, I feel in my heart that if God will help me, and the Presbyterian Church will help me, old master's little boy shall bless the dying man's race."

Some very eloquent and touching descriptions are given by the white men and women of the South, of their old mammies, into whose arms they were placed in earliest infancy, and whose lisping tongues were first taught by these dear old saints to speak the name of Jesus. Many of these aged ones are still dearly beloved and affectionately cared for by their old owners.

Among the slaves were often found many highminded and pious men and women. Bishop Hayward says some of the holiest men he ever knew were slaves. Some of the slave-preachers were men of great pulpit power, and enjoyed the confidence and sympathy of their white brethren in the ministry. Others of them had exalted ideas of their duty to God, and preached the Gospel at the risk of punishment from unsympathizing masters.

In the pine woods near Florence, South Carolina, I entered the humble cabin of a preacher. I was hundreds of miles away from my family, and could not see them for months to come. Said the wife, "I never was away from my husband but one time in all my life, when he was gone two weeks. When he come home it 'peared like I didn't had no sense, I was so glad." Princes and millionaires may well envy a devotion like this.

During the war the Government decided to enlist colored men in its service. The Records of the War Department show that there were 178,975 colored men who became soldiers of the United States. We have already made reference to the testimony of officers at Port Hudson as to their bravery in action.

The late General S. C. Armstrong, to whom reference has already been made, served two and a half years with negro soldiers. His experience as commander of the Ninth and Eighth Regiments of United States colored troops convinced him of the good qualities and capacities of the freedmen. "Their quick response to good treatment and to discipline was a constant surprise. Their tidiness, devotion to their duty and their leaders, their dash and daring in battle, and ambition to improve—often studying their spelling-books under fire—showed that they deserved as good a chance as any people." Similar testimonies have been given by many other commanders of colored troops.

There is no record at the War Department as to the number of colored soldiers that fell in action or died of wounds and disease. According to the latest official statistics, 67,058 officers and enlisted men of the Federal army were killed in action, and 292,470 died of wounds and disease in the late war.*

That the colored people have made great progress since they were emancipated, none can deny. The late Governor Brown, of Georgia, said: "The negroes have shown a capacity to receive education, and a disposition to elevate themselves that is exceedingly gratifying, not only to me, but to every right-thinking man." Bishop A. G. Haygood, of the Methodist Episcopal Church South, says: "The progress of the negro race in the United States during the past twenty years is one of the marvels of history." A distinguished Southern minister, familiar with the South from the Potomac to the Rio Grande, said on a public occasion: "Since God's sun has moved across the heavens, no race has made such progress in the same length of time

* See Note D.

as the colored people have made since they were set free."

Governor Northern, of Georgia, says that the negroes of his State pay taxes on $16,000,000, and the white people on $462,000,000. This gives a ratio of about one to twenty-nine. It has been stated, on what seems to be good authority, that the negroes of the whole South pay taxes on $264,000,000 worth of property.

The following statements from the Annual Report of the Auditor of Public Accounts for Virginia for the year 1893, show that where a colored man owns one dollar, a white man owns about thirty dollars. This report also shows that where a colored man pays one dollar for taxes, a white man pays not thirty dollars, but only about eleven dollars:

### Value of Personal Property—1893:

| | |
|---|---:|
| Total value........................................ | $93,838,414 00 |
| Total value owned by whites................. | 90,373,044 00 |
| Total value owned by negroes. .............. | 3,465,370 00 |

### Value of Real Estate:

| | |
|---|---:|
| Total value........................................ | $306,200,638 00 |
| Total value owned by whites................. | 296,371,055 00 |
| Total value owned by negroes................ | 9,829,583 00 |

### Taxes Assessed for 1893:

| | |
|---|---:|
| Whites.............................................. | $1,824,153 74 |
| Negroes............................................. | 172,391 28 |

They have made progress in education. They have now 1,500,000 children in school, while more

PROF. GEORGE RICE HOVEY, A. M.

than 2,500,000 have learned to read and write. When the writer first came to the South there were no colored teachers; now there are fully 25,000. At the close of the war there were few or no colored teachers in Virginia; now there are 2,041, of whom 1,130 are colored women. These teachers receive on an average $26.86 per month. At the close of the war there were but three colored physicians; now there are about 800. There were then only two colored lawyers; now there are about 300. There are about 200 editors of papers. There are 1,000 college-bred colored ministers, and 250 colored students in the universities of Europe. Those who wish to investigate this subject more thoroughly are referred to the following sources of information:

"Second Mohonk Conference on the Negro Question," Boston, 1891, 8vo.; "Twenty-two Years Work of Hampton Normal and Agricultural Institute," Hampton, 1891, 8vo.; "Education of the Negro," by W. T. Harris, Atlantic Monthly, Vol. LXIX (June, 1892), p. 721; "A Voice from the South," by a black woman of the South (A. J. Cooper), Ohio, 1892 (published by Aldine Printing House, Xenia, Ohio); "A Brief Historical Sketch of Negro Education in Georgia," by R. R. Wright, Savannah, Georgia, 1894; "Afro-American Press and its Editors," by I. G. Penn, Springfield, Massachusetts, 1891 (Willey & Company, Publishers);

"Condition of the Negro," by A. T. Smith and others, New York *Independent*, April 2, 1891; "Proceedings National Educational Association," 1880, p. 76, 1889, pp. 546–553, 1890, p. 497; "Twenty Years of Negro Education," by J. M. Keating, Popular Science Monthly, Vol. 28, p. 24.

For educational statistics, collegiate and professional, you may consult the Annual Reports of the Commissioner of Education, under head of "Education of the Colored Race," Vol. 2, for 1890–91, pp. 961, 1469.

## CHAPTER XV.

*Then—Now—Pleasant Recollections—Preaching to Phil. Kearney Post, G. A. R., and R. E. Lee Camp—Visits Abroad—Beneficiary Aid—The American Baptist Home Mission Society and its Workers.*

IT may be expected that I should say something about the *religious* progress of the colored man since he became free. I am aware that he has been the subject of many unkind remarks and many caricatures. His piety and integrity have been assailed, and newspaper correspondents have tried to create merriment by giving amusing reports of his public utterances and his sermons. It should be remembered that the list of words that the former slave knew was small, and therefore his efforts to pronounce many words used by the whites were not very successful. But his heart was right, and God signally honored the slave preachers in saving many souls. It is not surprising that a student should say: "I have come to insult you," when he meant "consult." It is not hard to understand how a man might pray before the sermon for the brother who was to "expand" the Gospel, when he meant to "expound" it. No affront was intended when the fervid brother prayed for a certain white man whom he looked upon as a friend of his race, and blessed the Lord that though this friend had a white skin, yet he had a *black* heart.

When the slaves were first made free the members of Baptist Churches were very much scattered. The white and colored were members of the same churches before the war, but at the close, in many instances, the churches were entirely broken up.

In Georgetown, South Carolina, the only white member that could be found was the clerk of the church, and he lived fourteen miles from the church edifice. The colored members, who were numerous, had mostly remained, but they could not act for the church. Conversions were occurring among them, and we organized a church and ordained a pastor. Some lived in out-lying districts, and the local leaders in those places could only indicate the number of their converts by a notch cut in a stick for every one who professed conversion under their leadership. Tin cups and tea cups were the vessels in which the wine was distributed at the communion. Frequently the places of worship were booths or arbors in the forests. The people were very poor. A marriage ceremony was performed, and the grateful groom, on the following morning, brought three eggs to reward the minister for his services.

Peculiar ideas prevailed as to hearing audibly the voice of God or of an angel at the time of conversion. For want of suitable words, often the most primitive, yet vivid, illustrations were used to express the experiences of the human soul in passing from darkness into light. When our School was in the Old Jail, one of our ministerial students, in giving an account of his conversion, after describing various exercises of mind, said: "All of a sudden a star busted in my breast, and I was mighty happy in the Lord." What language could more poetically describe the ecstatic emotions that burst in upon the soul when it passes from darkness into the light of the glorious Gospel of the son of God?

Some of the prayers and sermons of the colored leaders are remarkable, alike for the beauty of the thought and the vividness of expression. I have heard from the lips of colored men some of the finest word painting that ever fell from human lips.

The following is part of a prayer offered by a layman in the first African Church, Richmond, Virginia. It is without the abbrevations with which it was accompanied when delivered: "In this dark way of sin and death, while the loud thunders of thy wrath roll in majesty in the sinner's ears and the blaze of thy fury flashes all of a sudden before his eyes, send your brooding spirit like a dove through the storm and speak peace to his wretched soul before it is everlastingly too late. Show him the slippery rocks and the miry clay. Make him see that Satan follows fast, tripping at his heels, and hell yawns open to catch him when he falls. Oh! arrest him by the mighty power of thy grace. Pour down your mercy like rain from the summer clouds. Make him open his blind eyes to see the beauty of thy holiness a-shining in the face of your beloved Son, like the rainbow when the storm is done gone and passed away. Oh, thou great King of Glory who rides in the golden chariot in the New Jerusalem, above the sun, I beseech and pray you drive thy white horses down this way; and when the hoofs of the horses strike this lower world and the dashing wheels come in our sight, stop thy chariot at Washington city, and alight in loving kindness at the door of thy servant, the President Grant, and tell him exactly what to do. Sound the meaning of your will in the Congress halls, and tell the great men without their own asking how to serve their country best. Purge the hearts of the Senators and Representatives from the love of sin, and lead their stumbling feet from the snares of hell. Help them to remember thy servants in every sorrow and temptation, as Jesus remembers them. Thin out the desire of honor and the love of salary from their souls like suckers out of corn; and may your name be above every name, and thy kingdom come into the high places and the low, like the light of morning comes to the hills and the valleys the same. After leaving Washington city and taking thy time, drive your chariot down over the fields and rein up thy horses of fire at the capital of old Virginia, alight out at the Governor's door, and go into his house and tell him what things he ought to say, and show him what things he ought to do, like a father who instructs his own children."

This prayer, uttered with great fervor and with some of the words drawn out in musical tones that were indescribable, held breathless the congregation. The throne of grace was near and the souls of the people were blessed.

In those early days of pioneer work in the South, there were but few, if any, church buildings owned by the colored people. Now there are large and comfortable edifices which they have erected and paid for, at a cost of twenty, thirty, and even forty thousand dollars. There are flourishing Sunday-schools, Young Men's Christian Associations, and various Societies for the culture and development of the young people. There are now Academies, Colleges, Schools of Law, Medicine and Theology. There are also cultivated preachers and accomplished professional men. Dr. A. E. Dickinson, editor of the *Religious Herald,* says in the *Independent* (New York), March 7th, 1895: " The negroes of the South are doing as well as we have any right to expect under all the circumstances. Their progress in building fine churches and raising great amounts of money for various descriptions of religious work is truly wonderful. Northerners should come down among us and see it all with their own eyes, then they would know how to appreciate it."

These things are mentioned as showing what is possible. But after all that has been done, there are hundreds of thousands that have never been reached, and who need the helping hand.

While many thousands in the South still occupy the one-room cabin, yet many own good homes, costing from one thousand to six and eight thousand dollars. The prosperity of a people depends upon the condition of the home life. No race or nation can rise above the moral condition of its women. If they are indolent, and vain, and fond of frivolous amusement, the men will too readily conform to the prevailing notions. If, on the other hand, the women are noble and aspiring, and graced with every womanly virtue, the men will eagerly strive to become worthy of them. In some countries of Europe there exist much ignorance, superstition and degradation. But when one sees the women engaged in removing the offal of the cities, or loading railroad cars, or mixing and carrying mortar, he learns why so much wretchedness, superstition and crime exist.

The effect of the training received at our schools for girls is seen in the communities where the graduates of these schools labor. A pupil is at school brought in contact with new influences. She becomes acquainted with new methods of missionary and temperance work. She receives new impulses, and goes back to her home among the mountains or on the lowlands, full of enthusiasm. Her influence for good is seen every where. It is manifest in her immediate family, among her associates, in the Sunday-school and in the church. The pastor is stimulated in his efforts, and the whole community is blessed. In some instances her influence extends beyond her native land. A few years ago there was a colored girl ploughing cotton in Tennessee. She left the cotton field for the schoolroom. She took a course of medicine at Nashville, and after receiving her degree, she went to Africa, where she has been supporting herself as a Medical Missionary among the natives. The Methodist Episcopal Church has recently decided to give her an appointment under their Board of Missions.

In the course of twenty-seven years' work in Richmond, there is very little that is unpleasant to be remembered. The city officials, the Police and Fire Departments, and others have shown the deepest interest in the protection and preservation of our property.

While in Richmond, in addition to my appointed work, I have preached 614 sermons. Of this number seventy-nine have been to white congregations, and 208 to the First African Church.

The Richmond *Dispatch* of May, 1888, contained this announcement: "R. E. Lee Camp and the United Veterans will join Phil. Kearney Post in attendance upon a Memorial Sermon to be preached to-night at Grace Street Baptist Church by Rev. C. H. Corey, D. D." On entering the pulpit I found on my left Phil. Kearney Post, G. A. R., and on my right R. E. Lee Camp of Confederate Veterans, with a large congregation in addition. The text was Joshua i, 7. The situation, to say the least, was a peculiar one; the President of a school for colored people preaching in *Richmond* a memorial discourse on the Union dead, before Federal and Confederate soldiers. Within a radius of four miles were buried nearly 40,000 who fell in action, or died of wounds or disease in the late war.

On Memorial Day, May 30th, the veterans of both armies, the Blue and the Gray, marching to the music of the same fife and drum, joined in the morning in decorating the graves of the Federal dead at Seven Pines, and in the afternoon the graves of the Confederate dead at Hollywood. As "Chaplain of the day" for Phil. Kearney Post, it was my privilege to be present at both services.

In 1878 the Young Men's Christian Association of Richmond, sent me as a delegate to the International Convention of Young Men's Christian Associations, which convened in August, at Geneva, Switzerland. As showing what effect the method of Sabbath observance in Continental Europe has upon Christian people, I may mention that it was the custom of the Young Men's Christian Association of Geneva, to make steamboat excursions on the lake on Sunday afternoons.

Through the kindness of the Board of Trustees of the Seminary, and the Board of the Home Mission Society, in 1890, leave of absence was granted me for several months to visit the Orient. Egypt, Palestine, Damascus, Baalbek, Beyrout, Cyprus,

Smyrna, Ephesus, Athens, Corinth, Constantinople and a number of the capitals of Europe were embraced in this delightful journey.

From an inquiry made not long ago it was found that there were then more than 500 white men preparing for the ministry in (not all) the Baptist Academies, Colleges and Theological Seminaries of the United States, who were receiving aid, at the average cost of $100 per man, making in all $50,000 per annum. These young men are from the oldest and richest States, with the wealth of a century behind them.

In one of our oldest Seminaries at one time ninety per cent. of the students received beneficiary aid. In some of our best Seminaries now six out of seven are beneficiaries. If white men cannot get along without assistance, can we expect that colored men who have but recently come from slavery can do so? They are poor; some of them are homeless; some have aged parents (formerly slaves) dependent upon them. It has been found necessary, therefore, to render assistance to those that really needed it. The sum of $40,595.03 in cash has been expended in the payment of the board of ministerial students. This money has come, largely, by solicitation from Sunday-schools, churches and private individuals. Many have made great sacrifices, and have done so cheerfully, for the sake of putting into the field a properly equipped minister of Christ. One, who for years supported a student in our Institute, lived in a humble home near a New England village, and raised strawberries on her little homestead. I have found her in her fields toiling in the hot summer sun, in order that she might add to her earnings. She was accustomed to peddle her berries through the village, from a wheelbarrow propelled by her own hands. She supported a student for a number of years, at a cost of $50 per year.

Sometimes we have been in great straits. On one occasion, at the Christmas holidays, there were not five dollars in hand, and there were twenty men to be provided for until the close of the term in May. We made known, as we ever do, our wants to God, and he sent us means from unexpected sources to carry us through without incurring a debt. One hundred and twenty-five dollars of this came from an entire stranger beyond the sea. At various times we have had remarkable answers to our prayers, and blessed assurances that God was watching over this, his own work.

Before closing this chapter I desire to say something of the work of the American Baptist Home Mission Society, under whose auspices this and many other schools have been planted and fostered. Seven or eight schools had been founded up to the close of the administration of Secretary S. S. Cutting. The amount of work done by Dr. H. L.

Morehouse,* who succeeded Dr. Cutting, in thirteen years, up to the time when he resigned the General Secretaryship, seems almost incredible. The record of what was accomplished during his administration is not only inspiring, but thrilling. Nothing but nerves of iron, unflagging energy, tireless working, an exhaustless patience, and an ever abiding faith in the God who holds the key that unlocks the hearts of his servants, could have accomplished such results. During that period the number of missionaries increased from 238 to 1,053; the number of schools, from eight to twenty-seven. The receipts per year at the commencement of that period were $176,393.19, at the close $500,930. Endowments were secured, and all departments of the work were strengthened and enlarged. What man could have done grander work than this?

Rev. M. MacVicar, LL. D., formerly Chancellor of McMaster University, Toronto, Canada, is giving with indomitable energy the ripe fruits of long experience in educational work, to the upbuilding of the educational institutions of the Home Mission Society. His advice and cooperation have materially strengthened our work in Richmond.

General T. J. Morgan, our General Secretary, well known in all the land as a soldier, an educator, and as a public officer of the United States Government, with his large knowledge of affairs, is throw-

---

*See Note E.

ing his energies into the work of marshaling the Baptist forces of the land, and of leading them forward in the line of duty. Already we have learned how great is his solicitude, that not only our Seminary but all the schools under the care of the Society should be developed to the highest state of efficiency. Truly this is a trio of "tried and true" workers.

It is worthy of remark in this connection, that during the period of thirty years in the service of the Home Mission Society, not a single check from the now venerable ex-Treasurer J. M. Whitehead, or from the present efficient Treasurer J. G. Snelling, has failed to reach us on time; and none of our Monthly Reports have failed to reach the office in New York.

Dr. Morehouse, at Nashville, in 1888, in his memorable address, entitled "A survey of twenty-five years' work for the colored people of the South," pays a glowing tribute to the noble men and women who had given unsparingly of their means to help build up the schools in the South. In referring to Dr. Nathan Bishop, Mrs. Bishop, Mrs. Benedict, Deacon Holbrook Chamberlain, John D. Rockefeller and others, he says: "Their names, associated with these institutions and entrenched in the affections of the people, will be immortal. Nobler men and women than these were never found among the friends of any society." Dr. Morehouse, referring to the early laborers in the Southern field, continues: "No lives of ease have been lived, no perfunctory service rendered by these who, with a missionary spirit that in many cases matches that exhibited in any mission field of earth, have bent every energy of their being to the accomplishment of their tasks. What has it cost? Tell us who can, what it cost that hero, Harry Woodsmall, who consumed the last atom of vital force in absolute self-surrender to Christ and the least of his lowly brethren in the South. Tell us who can—for she will not tell it—what it has cost Joanna P. Moore in her twenty-five years continuous toil among the homes and the by-ways of the neglected and the needy. Tell us, who can—for never from the lips of these brave, uncomplaining souls do you hear a recital of it—what it has cost these veterans, whom we count it an honor to meet with us to-day, Drs. Philips and Corey, and Drs. Tupper and King, who could not be here! The cost in those earlier years, when the condition of things was vastly different from the present, is not only beyond computation but beyond apprehension. Had some of these wrought in a foreign land with corresponding results, their name and fame would have gone around the world."

## CHAPTER XVI.

*Slow Progress—Our Ancestors—The Bible—Work for the Lowly—Suffrage—Conclusion.*

SOMETIMES the complaint has been heard that the progress made by the colored people has not been sufficiently rapid. It should be remembered, however, that all history teaches that the uplifting process among races is slow. When Julius Cæsar invaded Britain in the year 55, B. C., he took some of the finest specimens of our savage ancestors to Rome. Cicero, in writing to his friend Atticus (see *Ad Atticum, Lib.* IV, 6), declared that none of them would be found fit to be a slave at Rome. It has taken 1900 years to change the descendants of these rude inhabitants of that little island to the noble specimens of Christian manhood and womanhood that we see in England and America to-day. In the days of the Cæsars it was the proudest boast a man could make, to say: "I am a Roman." What makes the difference between the descendant of him who was not fit to be a slave at Rome, and the ignorant and superstitious descendant of the proud Roman of the olden times? The pure teachings of the Bible is the answer. The Bible, not chained in cloisters, nor torn from the people and burned, but the Bible, open, and placed within the reach of the poorest and humblest inhabitant of the land, is the great lever to lift races and nations. Queen Victoria, when King Theodore, of Abyssinia, wrote to her, asking why England, so small a country, was yet so great, returned as her answer a Bible, with an autograph letter containing the following royal reply: " Your Majesty: *This book* has made my kingdom great, and will make great your majesty's kingdom also."

The growth towards righteousness and truth is slow. In the time of the Conquest it was the custom to buy men and women in all parts of England, and to carry them from Bristol to Ireland for sale. They sold as slaves their nearest relatives, and even their own children. (See *Life of Bishop Wolston.*)

The streets of London, now with its 4,300,000 inhabitants, were " foul and noisome," and unpaved until Henry VIII commenced the work of improving and paving them. This King had but one ship of war at the beginning of his reign with which to defend himself from his enemies. (See *Taine's English Literature*, Vol. I, 146.) Before the time of Elizabeth, A. D. 1558, the country houses of gentlemen were little more than straw-thatched cottages, plastered with the coarsest clay, and lighted only by trellises. They had no glass in their houses; they used a good round log for a bolster or pillow, and ate with wooden spoons. The moral condition of the people of those times was also deplorable.

Among the "meere" or wild Irish, in the year 1600, they were accustomed to fasten the plough to the horse's tail, and to burn the oats from the straw to save the trouble of threshing them. Acts of Parliament were passed against these practices. Their great lords dwelt in poor clay houses or cabins, of boughs covered with turf. In many parts women, as well as men, had even in the winter time only a linen rag about their loins, and a woolen mantle on their backs. They had no tables, but set their meat on a bundle of grass. They feasted on "fallen" horses, and drank milk warmed with a stone first cast into the fire (*Tylor's Primitive Culture*, Vol. I, 44).

Others are superstitious as well as the colored people. Martin Luther believed in witches, and he says: "I would have no pity on these witches; I would burn them all." The great and good Sir Matthew Hale hung witches in Suffolk county, on the authority of Scripture as he thought, and the consenting wisdom of all nations. King James, of England, presided at the torture of Dr. Fian, for bringing a storm against the king's ship on its course from Denmark, by the aid of a fleet of witches in sieves who carried out a christened cat to sea. Even Richard Baxter, of the "Saints Rest," believed in witches.

In Bohemia, a recent account (1864) says that the

fishermen do not venture to snatch a drowning man from the water; they fear that the "water-demon" would take away their luck in fishing, and drown themselves at the first opportunity. In short, other races have always had their superstitions, as well as the black race.

It has taken a long time to uproot many errors, superstitions, and immoralities from the nations now foremost in the march of civilization. The more of these that are removed, the greater is the safety to a commonwealth. As blood-poisoning is destructive to the whole human system, so the existence in our body politic of corrupt elements endangers our national life. If the stern of a ship goes down the prow will inevitably follow. If we in the South, who have so many millions among us yet in ignorance, do not lift them up, they will drag us and our children down.

The work of lifting up the masses must begin at the bottom. I have not been able to quite agree with my loved and honored friend, the late Dr. John A. Broadus,* whose present departure from earth is mourned by two hemispheres, that we must begin at the top and work downward in our educational and religious labors. It seems to me that if we lift the lowly, along with them we lift those above them. We put the fire under the boiler and not on the top. Wesley preached to the com-

---

*See Note F.

mon people of England—the horny-handed sons of toil. They were saved, uplifted; and along with them the corrupt and profligate nobility. Wesley lifted the crowds and saved England from a more bloody revolution than that which devastated France.

The efforts of the negroes to secure an education has, no doubt, been a stimulus to many white people. See the following interesting letter. J. B. Gambrell, D. D., President of Mercer University, Macon, Georgia, in writing to a Northern Baptist, makes the following statement. See *The Examiner* for March 14th, 1895:

"Last June I delivered a diploma to a preacher who had completed his studies at Mercer. The next day, in my office, he said : ' Do you know how I came to enter Mercer? It was in this way: I was preaching out in the country, and the people there said they thought I could beat two college men; but I was not satisfied. There was a feeling that I needed a much better training to do the work that was on me. One day I met a colored brother on the train, and he told me of his studies in the Atlanta School for colored preachers—how greatly he was helped, and he wound up by saying that he did not see how any preacher could be willing to go into the work without an education. When he got through, one thing was settled; I determined to go through Mercer. How, I did not know, but my purpose was fixed—to have an education.'"

Dr. Gambrell adds these significant words: "He is one of our best men; and how true it is that we cannot help the lowliest of our people without helping ourselves."

There is no doubt, that if not in this precise way then in some other way, the progress of the colored man has served as an incentive to his white neighbor.

The right of suffrage has been granted to the negro, and various opinions have been expressed concerning this matter. One distinguished minister of the South pronounces the giving of the right of suffrage "a blunder and a crime." Another representative man of national reputation, in a published article, writes as follows: "I approach what is to my apprehension the most unmatchable outrage ever inflicted by a civilized people. Some acts, like the partition of Poland, stand out on the pages of history as disgraceful national crimes; but most of them shade into minor offences compared with the crime-breeding, race-endangering, liberty-imperiling savagery of conferring the right of suffrage upon the negroes *en masse.* \* \* \* \* Giving the elective franchises to the suddenly-emancipated negroes, if not such a repeating crime, would be a farce for the ages."

The *Christian Advocate*, of Richmond, Virginia, in 1888, uses the following language: "We are ready to close our gates even to the European with

his genius and history, but decree it a sacrilege to hint that a creature out of a rude hut in a southern swamp, with mind, manners and motives hardly above a gorilla, is not fit to direct and dominate the 'first nation in the fore files of time.'"   *   *   *
"While the negro, whose native land is just across the Mediterranean from Athens and Rome, and along the same river with the wise Egyptians, yet, never rising out of sloven savagery in all the centuries, remaining a brute and bondman throughout the ages, is the ebon Czar of America, the sooty and grotesque idol of advanced statesmen. It makes men shudder for the sanity of our civilization."

It may seriously be questioned whether it is wise in men who reverently acknowledge God in all their ways (for the writers are gentlemen of high and devout Christian character) to express themselves so positively on a point like this. God, who knows the end from the beginning, permitted it, and He does not work simply for to-day. His plans run on and on through the eternities. The web he weaves is from everlasting to everlasting. He works down out of human sight, and the drapery of invisibility often enshrouds the Divine Arm. None but the God of nations knows what is in store for our republic. The tides of anarchy are already surging against the foundation stones of our social fabric. New and disintegrating foreign elements are already securing a foothold on our soil. Infidel and unprincipled men, doubtless will, at no distant day, undertake to control or overthrow all that we, as a nation, hold most dear. The colored man is not an anarchist, nor a Sabbath-breaker, nor a maker of drunkards. He speaks our own language; he loves our common Lord; he is loyal to our institutions. If we do our duty to him and prepare him to use intelligently his ballot, he and his posterity will be allies that may assist in saving our country from the perils that threaten to engulf it.

All the crimes and misdoings of our common humanity should not be placed at the door of the colored man. History tells of the diabolical cruelties of some whom the world calls its greatest heroes. The social life of the most civilized peoples has its scandals, even in the highest stations in life. Nefarious schemes for gain are planned; great gambling establishments exist; colossal defalcations occur; and breaches of trust are common among what are called the dominant races. It is not wise to arrogate to ourselves too much superior virtue, but with Christ's love in our hearts, like Peter who took the crippled man that lay at the Temple gate by the hand, we should take by the hand and lift up the despairing and helpless of every race, whether black, white, red or yellow, and whether they are in our own or in other lands.

What then is our duty? The crisis is upon us; the old regime is passing away; a new era is dawning upon us; the gates of the twentieth century will soon swing open before us. As Christians in America do we realize our responsibilities? Some one has said that the Baptists and Methodists of America are responsible for the development of the colored people, as so many of them belong to these denominations. As Baptists are we doing our duty? More than one-third of all the Baptists on the globe are found among the colored people of the South.

Our work of providing a trained ministry for the 1,500,000 colored Baptists of the South needs strengthening all along the line. Students are coming to our Seminary from the far South, the West Indies, British Honduras, and from Africa. These need aid. Our "*Faith Fund*" is sometimes very low. Who will make provision for the support of a student in our Seminary *for all time?* Who will erect a memorial for himself or his family more enduring than granite or bronze, by founding a Scholarship? Men have erected monuments and built mausoleums to perpetuate their names. But the tombs and pyramids of earth have been rifled by ruthless robbers, and the dust of Pharaohs and Kings has been scattered to the winds of heaven. Monumental cities and temples are in ruins. But whenever a steward of God sends a fully equipped and consecrated man into the world, he will live in him until the end of time. It is better to build in MEN than to build in marble.

# NOTES.

### NOTE A.—MAJOR-GENERAL ANDERSON.

The following is from the Adjutant-General's office, Washington, D. C., August 15, 1893:

"SIR: In answer to your communication of the 11th instant, the following information is furnished from the files of this office: Fort Sumpter, S. C., was surrendered April 14, 1861, by Major Robert Anderson, 1st Artillery, and the United States flag was raised again on that fort April 14, 1865, by the same officer, who at that time held the rank of Brigadier-General and Brevet Major-General on the retired list.

"Ordinance Sergeant James Kearney, United States Army, was present at Fort Sumpter at its surrender in 1861, and at the raising of the United States flag there in 1865."

### NOTE B.—VALUE OF PROPERTY DESTROYED.

In the Richmond *Whig* of April 10, 1865, there is a partial list of the owners of real estate destroyed in the fire, and of the property respectively owned by them. The figures represent the assessed value in 1860. The amount given in that list, which is only a partial one, is $2,146,240. Says the *Whig:* "Imposing as these figures appear, they are far short of the truth, for the reason already stated, that real estate was, before the war, invariably assessed much below the value it would have commanded in the market. Our list covers no more than the value of the bricks and mortar destroyed." * * * "In addition to the buildings, &c., destroyed are the Public Warehouse, in which was stored a very large quantity of tobacco; the Richmond and Petersburg railroad bridge; the Richmond and Danville railroad bridge, two spans of which were destroyed, and Mayo's passenger bridge." Add to these losses the many public buildings owned by the Confederacy, the Government stores, and the contents of the stores of merchants, and the loss will be seen to be enormous. One warehouse alone contained 1,500 hogsheads of tobacco.

NOTE C.—BREVET BRIGADIER-GENERAL S. C. ARMSTRONG.

General S. C. Armstrong was born in the Sandwich Islands in 1839 of parents who were missionaries. In 1860 he left that country to complete his education at Williams College, Massachusetts. He served in the late war two and one-half years with negro soldiers. General O. O. Howard, Commissioner of the Freedmen's Bureau, in 1866, placed him in charge of ten counties in Eastern Virginia, with headquarters at Hampton. In 1868 he commenced the educational work at Hampton which has been so successful. He died in May, 1893, his death no doubt being hastened by the weight of his cares and the intensity with which he devoted himself to his duties.

NOTE D.—THE NORTHERN SOLDIERS.

The entire number who enlisted during the war, when reduced to a three years' standard, was, 2,324,516.

In the various National Cemeteries, of which there are eighty-two, there are interred 331,755. The names of 149,913 of these are unknown. Of these interments about 9,300 are Confederates.

A writer in one of our prominent daily papers a few weeks ago speaks of "the Anglo-Saxon of the North aided by his hords of foreign hirelings brought from every clime to destroy us," &c.

For the information of the writer of the above, and all who may have a similar impression, I give the following percentage of the nationalities of those who enlisted in the Northern army from 1861 to 1865. It is taken from the New York *Sun* of August 30, 1891:

|                      | Per cent. |
| --- | --- |
| Native Americans     | 75.48 |
| Germans              | 8.76 |
| Irish                | 7.14 |
| British Americans    | 2.60 |
| English              | 2.26 |
| Other foreigners     | 3.76 |

The percentage of native Americans who deserted was five; of all others, seventy-five.

### Note E.—H. L. Morehouse, D. D.

Since his resignation as Corresponding Secretary, Dr. Morehouse still serves the Home Mission Society as its efficient Field Secretary. He reminds me that Dr. Lathrop and J. B. Hoyt, who are spoken of on page 36, as coming to Charleston, South Carolina, in 1865, "were appointed by the American Baptist Home Mission Society to make this Southern visit." See page 424 of the *Jubilee Volume* of the Society, by H. L. Morehouse, for an account of their reception.

### Note F.—John A. Broadus, D. D., LL.D.

This distinguished scholar, President of the Southern Baptist Theological Seminary, died at Louisville, Kentucky, March 16th, 1895. He was a ripe scholar, a rare instructor, and a charming preacher. He was a polished gentleman, with an indescribable charm of manner that drew all hearts to him. Well does the writer remember a conversation with him while walking to the church one afternoon during the session of the Southern Baptist Convention in Baltimore. Familiarly drawing his arm under mine he expressed his hearty sympathy with me in my work, and cordially encouraged me to command his services in any way and at any time I might desire.

The following is from the *Courier-Journal*, Louisville, Kentucky:

"Dr. Broadus' last appearence at the General Association of

Kentucky Baptists was to make a plea for colored preachers. Dr. McRidley, a colored teacher, had made a plea for his normal school, at Cadiz; the matter was about to be passed without favorable action; Dr. Broadus took the floor and said: 'Let us have a collection;' and although a little objection was made, he carried the day, as was his way. He went through the church and collected the money in his own hat. On another occasion, at the Southern Baptist Convention, when he spoke of the Home Board, he said of the colored people:

"'Heaven help me, I shall say nothing of the race problem or any other problem. You can't solve a problem by wholesale. You can only do it as Nehemiah did when he rebuilt the walls of Jerusalem—each do his part. The Scriptures say: "As ye have opportunity do good toward all men." We have an opportunity. Let us do the colored people good. Let no unkind criticism dishearten. \* \* \* \* As to what is proper I cannot lay down any law; but whatever you or I can do, oh! God of mercy, help you and me to do. One of the heaviest responsibilities, one of the highest duties that God Almighty ever gave you and me was to do what we could for the elevation of the colored people.'"

In a letter to the *Religious Herald*, Dr. Broadus bears a delicate and generous testimony to the work accomplished by our School in Richmond. Drs. Manly, Boyce and Broadus, all of whom I visited in their homes at Louisville, have rested from their labors and their works do follow them. These, with Dr. Williams, their colleague, have all passed away since I commenced my work in Richmond, twenty-seven years ago.

# INDEX.

Abbott, Rev. M. S. G. (M. D.)........... 137
American Baptist Home Mission Society,
      36, 48, 52, 65, 66, 73, 77, 90, 111, 113, 127, 128, 216
American Baptist Publication Society.................... 150
Acadia University.................................. 13
Aid to Students.................................... 215
Alexandria........................................ 18
Anderson, Major..........................25, 32, 229
Anderson, Rev. P. E................................ 151
Anderson, Rev. Spotswood A........................ 141
Answers to Prayer................................. 216
Armstrong, General S. C..................123, 202, 230
Augusta Institute..........................39, 40, 58

Backus, J. S. (D. D.)................................. 66
Bacote, Rev. S. W. (B. D.)........................... 171
Bailey, Lieutenant-Colonel Joseph.................... 18
Banks, General................................ 17, 19
Beecher, Rev. Henry Ward......................32, 33
Benedict, Mrs..................................... 218
Bennett, Colonel................................... 23
Berkeley, Rev. Reuben............................. 139
Bill, Hon. Henry................................83, 84
Binney, J. G. (D. D.).........................52, 53, 107
Bishop, Nathan (LL.D.).........................20, 218
Bishop, Rev. P. P................................. 113
Board of Trustees, Meeting of...................... 128
Boykin, Rev. M.................................... 37
Boykin, Rev. J. W................................. 171
Broadus, John A. (D. D.)..................198, 223, 231

Brockenton, Rev. I. P. .................. 39, 79, 115, 142, 162
Brouner, Dr. ........................................ 16
Brown, Rev. A. J. ................................. 166
Brown, Rev. J. S. ........................... 144, 146
Building Fund ..................................... 183
Burrows, J. L. (D. D.) ............................. 46

Callahan, Rev. P. H. .............................. 171
Canby, General ................................... 120
Carey, Lott ...................................... 196
Chahoon, Mayor George ............................ 121
Chamberlain, Deacon H ............................ 218
Charleston ......................... 20, 21, 31, 36, 44
Chase, Dr. ........................................ 16
Chick, Rev. T. J. ................................. 150
Chisholm, Rev. A. (D. D.) ......................... 160
Claflin University ................................. 38
Coffin, C. C. ............................. 7, 42, 44, 46
Coleman, Rev. C. S. .............................. 155
Coles, Rev. J. J. ........................... 158, 159
Colley, Rev. W. W. ............................... 143
Colver Institute ................................... 88
Colver, Nathaniel (D. D.) .... 54–58, 60–63, 72, 73, 75, 76, 78, 86
Conant, J. T. (D. D.) ............................. 182
Conway, Chaplain T. M ............................. 15
Cosby, Rev. Solomon .............................. 145
Cousins, Rev. William ............................. 141
Cramp, J. M. (D. D.) ....................... 14, 113, 114
Crawley, E. A. (D. D.) ......................... 13, 14
Curry, Hon. J. L. M. ............................. 119
Cutting, S. S. (D. D.) .................... 101, 102, 216
Cyrus, Rev. J. H. A ............................... 153

Davis, Jefferson ............................... 42, 43
David, Rev. W. J. .......................... 145, 148
De Laney, Dr. ..................................... 30
Dickerson, Rev. H. W ............................. 141

## INDEX.

Dickinson, A. E. (D. D.) .................................... 118
Duers, Rev. Henry E. .................................... 137

Ellyson, Mayor H. K. ............................... 119, 121
Everts, W. W. (D. D.) .................................... 181

Field, S. W. (D. D.) ............................... 116, 117
First African Baptist Church ............................ 73
Fort Wagner. ............................................. 21, 23
Freedmen's Bureau, The. ................... 81, 87, 93, 123
Fulton, J. D. (D. D.).. .................................. 53, 65

Gambrell, J. B. (D. D.) .................................. 224
Gardner, Sterling ......................................... 137
Garland, Rev. S. A ....................................... 162
Garrison, William Lloyd ................................... 33
Gassaway, Rev. E. V. ..................................... 170
General Assembly, Act of........................... 130, 131
Goodman, Miss H. W. ..................... 59, 66, 69, 82-84
Gordon, Rev. C. W. B. .................................... 159
Govan, J. Corey .................................... 108, 109
Grant, General ............................................. 44
Gregory, Rev. Joseph ..................................... 144
Griggs, Rev. A. R. ....................................... 165
Guinness, Henry Grattan (D. D.) .......................... 182

Hamilton, Rev. James ...................................... 36
Hardee, General ........................................... 23
Hartshorn Memorial College ............................... 135
Hayden, Rev. Lucius E. (D. D.) ............................ 40
Haygood, Bishop A. G. .............................. 201, 203
Heriot, W. J .............................................. 34
Hilton Head ............................................ 29, 34
Holmes, Rev. James H. ...... 55, 63, 78, 79, 86, 138, 196, 197
Hovey, Alvah (D. D.) .................................... 181
Hovey, George Rice (A. M.) ............................... 179

Howard, General O. O. .................................. 123
Howson, Dean....................................... 182
Hoyt, J. B........................... 36, 104, 182, 183
Hoyt, U. G............................................ 103, 126
Hughes, W. N......................................... 34

Indianola. ............................................ 15

Jackson, Rev. George W............................. 140
Jeter, J. B. (D. D.)................................. 118
Johnson, Rev. W. T. (B. D.) ........................ 172
Jones, John William (D. D.)......................... 119
Jones, Rev. Joseph Endom (D. D.)............... 174-178
Jorden, Rev. Nelson................................. 144
Jubilee Celebration................................. 30

Kelly, Judge......................................... 33
King, Dr............................................. 219
King Theodore, Letter to............................ 221

Labors of Students.................................. 136
Lathrop, Edward (D. D.) .................... 36, 113, 182
Legare, Rev. Jacob.................................. 39
Lewis, Rev. P. S. (B. D.)........................... 168
Lewis, T. Willard............................... 38, 114
Lewis, Rev. Z. D. (B. D.) .......................... 167
Library Fund......................................... 183
Lincoln, President................................... 46
Loan Fund, D. Henry Sheldon......................... 184
Lumpkin's Jail................... 47, 54, 69, 73, 74, 80, 82, 86
Lumpkin, Mr.................................... 42, 43, 76

MacVicar, Rev. M. (LL. D.).......................... 217
Madison, Rev. Henry................................. 162
Madison University............... 49, 50, 84, 176, 178
Mahan, Commander.................................... 18

## INDEX.   237

Matamoras ............................................ 15
Matthews, Rev. J. B. .................................. 140
Manly, Rev. R. M. ..................................... 87
Mayo, A. D. (D. D.) ................................... 21
McDaniel, Rev. Charles H. ............................ 139
McFadden, Hon. Orren .................................. 17
Moore, Joanna P. ..................................... 219
Morehouse, H. L. (D. D.)........102–104, 127, 183, 216, 218, 231
Monument to a Slave................................... 200
Morgan, General T. J. ............................184, 217
Morris, Harvey ....................................... 109
Morris Island ...............................20, 23, 24, 26
Mower, Rev. Mr ........................................ 48

National Theological Institute.............39, 53, 58, 60, 64, 65
Negro Education, Sources of Information on..........205, 206
Newman, Rev. A. M. .................................... 48
New Orleans........................................15, 19
Newton Theological Institution......................... 14
Nichols, Mrs. Sarah Hanson ............................ 84
Northen, Governor .................................... 204
Northern Soldiers.................................203, 230

Old African Church, History of......................185–196

Parker, J. W. (D. D.) ............... 57, 59, 61, 67, 68, 85, 112
Pawley, J. C. ......................................... 39
Payne, Rev. C. H. (D. D.) ............................ 157
Payne, Rev. E. ..............................163, 165, 197
Pease, Captain.....................................16, 17
Peck, Solomon (D. D.) ......................54, 57, 59, 65
Pegues, Rev. A. W. (Ph. D.) .......................... 155
Perry, Rev. Elisha ................................... 153
Philips, Dr. .......................................... 219
Pickens, Governor. .................................... 26
Pierce, Rev. D. M. (A. M.) ........................... 156
Port Hudson .......................................15, 17

Powell, Rev. Guy............................................. 152
Preaching to Phil. Kearney Post........................ 213
Presley, Rev. J. H............................................. 158
Professorships................................................. 183

Quarles, Rev. R. C............................................ 162

Reed, Lieutenant.............................................. 28
Religious Herald.................................52, 55, 170
Religious Progress of the Negro..................207–211
Removal, Efforts for......................................... 184
Reports of Auditor in Virginia.......................... 204
Richmond, Evacuation of ................................. 42
Richmond Institute, Incorporated................124–126
Richmond Theological Seminary................37, 130
Richmond Whig..........................................44, 45
Rio Grande....................................................... 15
Robert, J. T. (LL.D.)......................................... 40
Robinson, Rev. C. G......................................... 170
Robinson, E. G. (D. D.) .................................... 181
Robinson, Rev. W. M........................................ 149
Rockefeller, J. D............................104, 183, 218
Ryland, Robert (D. D.)...........55–58, 62, 193–196

Samson, G. W. (D. D.) ..................................... 65
Sanders, Rev. Sancho........................................ 37
Sawyer, Rev. A. W. (D. D., LL.D.)..................... 14
Savannah, Fall of ............................................. 23
Scholarships..................................................... 183
Scruggs, Rev. L. A. (M. D.)............................... 154
Seabrook, N. H................................................. 14
Sermons Preached in Richmond....................... 213
Seymour, Lieutenant R. G............................15, 16
Shaw, Colonel................................................... 21
Sherman, General............................................. 23
Simmons, Rev. J. B. (D. D.)........65, 69, 87, 90–100, 106
Simmons, W. J. (D. D.)..................................... 178

Slave, A Faithful.................................................. 199
Slaveholder's Son, Testimony of......................... 200
Smith, S. F. (D. D.) ....................................114, 115
Smith, W. H ................................................... 82
Snelling, J. G.................................................. 218
Soldiers, Colored.........................................16, 203
Soldiers, White................................................ 203
Southern Baptist Convention............................. 145
Spiller, Rev. Richard........................................ 138
Stone, Marsena (D. D.)..................................... 181
Stuart, Prof. A. P. S ........................................ 14
Suffrage, Right of............................................ 225
Supreme Court of Appeals................................. 121

Taliaferro, Rev. G. L. P...............................160, 161
Taylor, E. E. L. (D. D.)..................................... 101
Teachers, List of.............................................. 173
Teague, Colin.................................................. 196
Thomas, L., Brigadier-General........................... 16
Thompson, George............................................ 32
Tilton, Theodore.............................................. 33
Tolman Fund, The Lydia S................................. 183
Turner, J. H. (B. D.)......................................... 169
Tupper, Dr...................................................... 219

Ullman, General Daniel..................................... 17
Uncle Jeffrey..........................................63, 84, 85
United States Christian Commission.......15, 20, 28, 34
United States Hotel..................................77, 80, 86

Value of Property destroyed.........................44, 229
Vassar, David Nathaniel (D. D.)....................178, 179
Visits Abroad.................................................. 213

Waldron, Rev. J. Milton..............................156, 157
Wales, Rev. L. W............................................ 161

Washington, Rev. Forris J.............................. 167
Waterhouse, C. W.........................................115, 116
Watts, Rev. Ellis (B. D.)................................. 168
Webster, Dr. A............................................ 38
Weitzel, General.......................................... 44
Wells, Rev. Aaron......................................... 151
Wells, Richard....................63, 78, 79, 86, 140, 197
Wheeler, Rev. E. S.....................................15, 16, 17
White, Rev. Dr............................................ 105
Whitehead, J. M........................................... 218
Whiting, Rev. Z. Taylor................................... 169
Winkler, Rev. E. T. (D. D.)..........................39, 111
Witches, Belief in........................................ 222
Woodsmall, Harry.......................................... 219

www.ingramcontent.com/pod-product-compliance
Lightning Source LLC
Chambersburg PA
CBHW021403230426
43666CB00006B/619